RONALD REAGAN

T R E A S U R E S

RONALD REAGAN

T R E A S U R E S

THE LIFE *of the* GREAT COMMUNICATOR
in PHOTOS & MEMORABILIA

RANDY ROBERTS AND DAVID WELKY

THUNDER BAY
P·R·E·S·S

San Diego, California

Thunder Bay Press
An imprint of Printers Row Publishing Group
10350 Barnes Canyon Road, Suite 100, San Diego, CA 92121
www.thunderbaybooks.com

Thunder Bay Press is an imprint of Printers Row Publishing Group, a division of Readerlink Distribution Services, LLC. The Thunder Bay Press name and logo are trademarks of Readerlink Distribution Services, LLC.

All notations of errors or omissions should be addressed to Thunder Bay Press, Editorial Department, at the above address. All other correspondence (author inquiries, permissions) concerning the content of this book should be addressed to becker&mayer! Books, 11120 NE 33rd Place, Suite 101, Bellevue, WA 98004.

Ronald Reagan Treasures is produced by
becker&mayer! Book Producers, Bellevue, Washington.
www.beckermayer.com

Editor: Sara Addicott
Designer: Rosanna Brockley
Photo researchers: Donna Metcalf and Jake Clifford
Production coordinator: Tom Miller

Publisher: Peter Norton
Publishing Team: Lori Asbury, Ana Parker, Laura Vignale
Editorial Team: JoAnn Padgett, Melinda Allman, Dan Mansfield
Production Team: Blake Mitchum, Rusty von Dyl

ISBN: 978-1-62686-441-2

Printed in China
19 18 17 16 15   1 2 3 4 5

CONTENTS

CHAPTER 1

"HE LOOKS LIKE A FAT LITTLE DUTCHMAN"

"HE POSSESSED A SENSE OF PRESENCE . . . A SENSE OF REALITY. HE FIT INTO ANY KIND OF ROLE YOU PUT HIM IN."

—RONALD REAGAN'S HIGH SCHOOL DRAMA COACH

There was no silver spoon in Ronald Wilson Reagan's mouth when he was born in a second-story bedroom above a general store and bakery on February 6, 1911. Nor did he make an easy entrance into the world. Outside, a blizzard blew shards of ice against the window, while inside the bedroom a midwife worked to deliver the child. After twenty-four hours of labor, Reagan finally arrived. He was the second son born to John Edward Reagan and Nelle Wilson Reagan.

Family legend maintains that when Reagan's father first saw his son, who was blue from screaming, he exclaimed, "For such a little bit of a fat Dutchman, he sure the hell makes a lot

Portrait of the Reagans: Jack and Nelle with their sons Neil (left) and Ronald. The future president looks as if he couldn't have been happier, an attitude he displayed all his life.

of noise." (Reagan changed the story a bit in his 1990 autobiography *An American Life,* writing that his father commented, "He looks like a fat little Dutchman. But who knows, he might grow up to be president someday.") His mother, weak from the hard delivery, answered, "I think he's perfectly wonderful." The exchange christened Ronald with the nickname "Dutch" and provided the first indication of his mother's high regard for him.

Tampico, the tiny Illinois town where Reagan took his first breaths, was off the beaten path of the growing country, tucked away in the heart of Middle America. Like the town itself, the child's parents were unassuming and undistinguished—good people and well liked, but without any claim to a wider fame.

John, whom everyone called Jack, was a gregarious Irish American—handsome and talkative, a natural salesman. Some of Reagan's biographers have compared Jack to Willie Loman, the tragic salesman in Arthur Miller's *Death of a Salesman.* Like Loman, Jack was a planner and a dreamer, always sure that somewhere in the future he would prosper in the shoe business. But he was never quite so beaten down as Willie Loman.

More than that, Jack Reagan had an intuitive feel and sympathy for working Americans. Dutch wrote that his dad was "a sentimental Democrat, who believed fervently in the rights of the workingman" but "never lost his conviction that the individual must stand on his own two feet." Jack believed in the equality of all men and put those

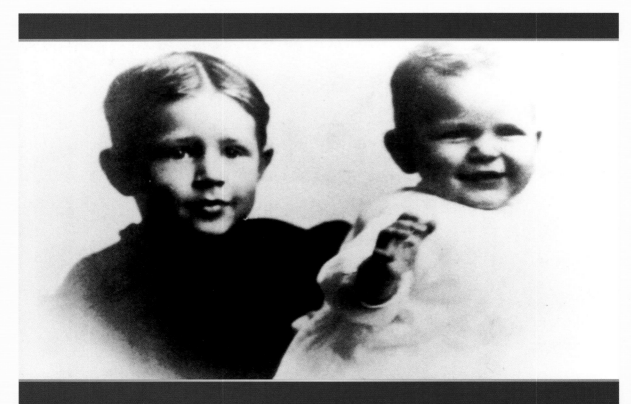

Ronald Reagan, age one, with his brother Neil. Young Dutch had rosy cheeks and a rosy disposition.

principles into action in his own life. When the popular film *The Birth of a Nation* came to town, Jack refused to allow Dutch and his older brother, Neil, to go to the theater. "It deals with the Ku Klux Klan against the colored folks," he explained, "and I'm damned if anyone in this family will go see it."

Jack's vice was the bottle. Although he probably drank too much for the small-town Midwestern gossips' comfort (and certainly too much for his strongly prohibitionist wife), he was a good father and husband. One cold winter evening, eleven-year-old Dutch returned home to find his father stretched out dead drunk on the front porch. He wanted to step over his dad, to pretend he had never seen him, and to head straight to bed. But seeing his father "spread out as if he were crucified," his hair wet from the snow, the son knew he had to get him into the house. And in that moment, Dutch accepted responsibility for his father. It was an important memory he carried with him into adulthood. "If we don't accept [responsibility] (and some don't), then we must just grow older without quite growing up."

Nelle Reagan was the heart of the family, and a lifelong source of inspiration for Dutch. Less than a year before she gave birth to him, she converted to the Christian Church (Disciples of Christ), fully embracing its mission. She gave her time to charitable causes, and focused her energies on producing religious plays and giving inspirational readings. In his first autobiography, Reagan

This formal photograph of Jack Reagan looks like a snapshot from the world of *The Magnificent Ambersons*. And like the Ambersons, he confronted his own personal struggles.

wrote that his mother "had the conviction that everyone loved her just because she loved them. My father's cynicism never made the slightest impression on her, while I suspect her sweetness often undermined his practical viewpoint of the world." Like her husband, she had little formal education. Both thought there were many things in life more important than academic degrees. Dutch's mother held that "no diploma was needed for kindness," and his father believed "energy and hard work were the only ingredients needed for success."

The attributes of both parents shaped Reagan's optimistic, easygoing, deceptively ambitious approach toward life. But as a youth, Dutch was more of a mama's boy. He went to church each Sunday with Nelle, watching her give dramatic religious readings before the congregation. And he accompanied her to the Dixon State Hospital, where they entertained patients. Nelle played the banjo and Dutch recited inspirational passages. These early performances introduced him to the pleasures of acting.

Dutch and his brother Neil's (nicknamed Moon) early lives were as peripatetic as a traveling salesman's. Whenever their dad lost a job or found a new opportunity, the family packed up and moved, mostly around northwestern Illinois. When Dutch was three, the family moved to Chicago; when he was four, they relocated to Galesburg. In the next few years they lived in Monmouth, again in Tampico, and in Dixon. Although they stayed put for many years in Dixon, they moved restlessly from house to house, usually because of Jack's precarious financial position. Jack, it turned out, was better at dreaming about success than achieving it.

The relocations and economic uncertainty, combined with Jack's drinking and Nelle's fervent religiosity, might have turned Dutch Reagan into an insecure, withdrawn boy. Instead, he developed, biographer Lou Cannon said, "a relentless optimism" that would define every aspect of his personality and future career.

After he became a politician, Reagan liked to begin talks with the parable of the two brothers: one a sky-is-falling pessimist and the other a boundless optimist. Seeking to balance the extreme personality traits of their sons, their parents consulted a psychiatrist. Following the expert's advice, they put the pessimist in a room full of expensive new toys, and the optimist in a room with a pile of horse manure and a shovel. When the parents returned to check on the boys some time later, they found the pessimist crying, afraid that if he played with the toys he would surely break one. The optimist, on the other hand, was up to his waist in manure, digging for all he was worth. Smiling at his parents, he said, "With this much manure around, I know there's a pony in here somewhere."

All his life Ronald Reagan would search for the pony, and over the years he would find a stable of them.

A SMALL-TOWN BOYHOOD

In Dixon, he found a classic Midwestern hometown—and so much more. In the center of dairy country, Dixon was a county seat of fewer than ten thousand people in a county of fewer than thirty thousand. Farmers and dairymen shopped along its quaint Main Street, and many of its local citizens worked in its Borden milk-condensing plant or the Grand Detour Plow Company. It was a place where virtually everybody knew everybody else,

left Dutch Reagan's boyhood home in Dixon, Illinois. This small town in the Midwest suited him quite well, and he retained a deep affection for Dixon throughout his life.

below A distinctive arch welcomed visitors to Dixon.

Ronald "Dutch" Reagan (far left in the second row) in fourth grade. Smaller than most of the other boys, he was friendly, outgoing, and well liked.

Young Reagan (hand on chin in front row) poses with other family members: Neil (front row, on right), Jack (middle row, on left), and Nelle (last row, second from left). It was the Jazz Age in America, but the pace of life in Dixon was considerably slower.

and nobody's secrets stayed secret for very long. Undoubtedly some people found Dixon backward and stifling.

But not Dutch Reagan. To him it was "the place to go back to," a small town to which he always felt indebted. After he made it in Hollywood—in the years before World War II, if you made it in Hollywood, you had really *made it*—he returned to Dixon to honor gossip columnist Louella Parsons, another local citizen who had earned fame in Hollywood, and to attend the premiere of the Warner Bros. film *International Squadron*. He was joined by such stars as Bob Hope, Ann Rutherford, and George Montgomery, who had traveled by train to Dixon. The *Chicago Herald-American* used the opportunity to affirm that the American dream was still alive. This "slice of Americana in the heart of the country," the reporter claimed, provided "a simple beginning" and "a stepping stone to success." Dutch called the event a "dream which probably every boy has at some time—that of coming home and being acclaimed by the home folks."

The Dixon of Reagan's boyhood was cut in half by the Rock River, and had enough patches of woods to entertain him for hours each day. He had no need for companions. The chirping birds, the rustling wind through the trees, the burbling of the river—the sounds and variations of nature thrilled him. He described his early years as "one of those rare Huck Finn–Tom Sawyer idylls," a time of hunting and fishing, and running and swimming. For the rest of his life, he enjoyed the pleasures of a walk along a river or the ocean, or a horse ride in the mountains or through high grass.

In Dixon, Dutch discovered the pleasure of reading. He learned to read early. When he was five, he could read newspapers, and by the time he was in elementary school, he demonstrated a gift for memorization. Reading opened the world for him. Before his tenth birthday he acquired a library card and frequently visited the book-lined "house of magic." The books he checked out and read were not surprising choices. Like other boys of his

Reagan at twelve years old. Already he knows how to strike a confident pose. In the coming years he would lose the knickers but not the attitude.

age—or older—he was drawn to adventure stories: Zane Grey's Westerns, James Fenimore Cooper's Leatherstocking Tales, Alexandre Dumas's stories of French heroics, Edgar Rice Burroughs's John Carter series, and Sir Arthur Conan Doyle's historical romances.

Some of the books Dutch devoured seemed to speak directly to him. Horatio Alger wrote dozens of books about boys from disadvantaged backgrounds who got ahead by pluck and luck. Harold Bell Wright, perhaps the most popular writer of the early twentieth century, penned inspirational tales that mixed self-improvement with Christian themes of redemption. The future president may have been particularly influenced by Wright's *That Printer of Udell's: A Story of the Midwest*. Dick Falkner, the protagonist of the novel, is the son of an alcoholic father who joins the Disciples of Christ Church, succeeds in business, marries well, moves into a life of public service, and discovers he has the oratorical ability to influence fellow citizens. By the end of the novel he has been elected to the U.S. Congress and is off to Washington, D.C., to enter "a field of wider usefulness."

As important as the public library was to Dutch, he was far from a bookish youth. With his remarkable memory, schoolwork came easily to him, but he did not strive for academic distinction. Instead, he worked to become a good athlete. In the late 1910s and early 1920s, college football was the rage in America. Boys in the Midwest, especially ones with connections to the Catholic Church

(Dutch's father and brother were Catholics), passionately cheered for Knute Rockne's Notre Dame teams. This was the age of the legendary George Gipp, called by Rockne "the most versatile player I've ever seen," later brought to life in Hollywood by Reagan himself in *Knute Rockne, All American*. It was the time of the equally celebrated Four Horsemen, who inspired Grantland Rice to pen one of the most memorable passages in sports journalism: "Outlined against a blue-gray October sky, the Four Horsemen rode again. In dramatic lore they are known as Famine, Pestilence, Destruction and Death. These are only aliases. Their real names are Stuhldreher, Miller, Crowley and Layden." In the 1920s, if you had a nickname like Dutch or Moon, you wanted to excel on the gridiron.

Dutch's brother, Moon, was an outstanding player. Dutch was run-of-the-mill, remembered more for his courage and determination than his talent. Poor eyesight effectively limited his potential. Playing tackle and end, he gave it his best and eventually became a starter in his senior year of high school, but the team won only two of nine games.

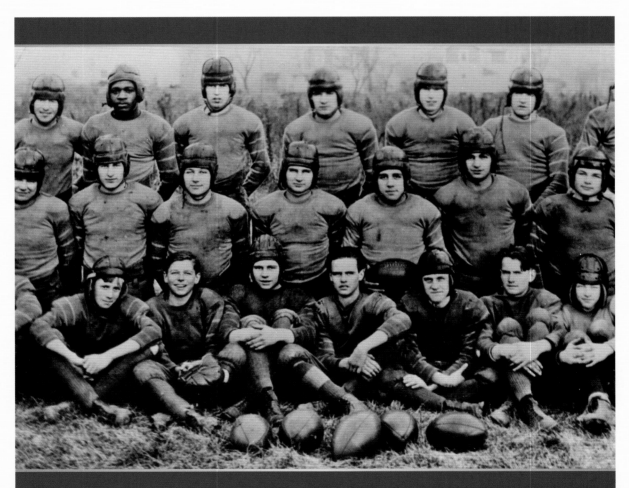

Eye problems and size prevented Reagan (front row, second from left) from excelling in football, but he loved the sport and impressed his coaches with his positive attitude. He eventually became a starter, but the team failed to achieve much success.

Dutch Reagan's 1927 high school yearbook photo.

"IT WAS LIKE A STAGE"

His best sport was swimming, even though he considered it more of a casual activity and a form of exercise than the more serious team sports of football, basketball, and baseball. He had learned to swim in the Rock River, a tributary of the Mississippi, an often dangerous stretch of the river. Drownings were common. But Dutch became an excellent swimmer, and in the summer of 1927, he became a lifeguard at Lowell Park, a spot on the Rock River close to Dixon. It was a position he held for six summers, from the age of sixteen to twenty-one.

Lowell Park was a particularly dangerous spot for swimmers. Downstream from a dam, the river's currents became roiling and treacherous when the sluices were opened. Its bottom had a sharp drop-off not far from the shore. During his years as a lifeguard, Dutch saved seventy-seven floundering bathers from drowning. Often the local newspaper trumpeted his heroics. "Pulled from the Jaws of Death," read one headline, describing how Reagan dove into the river after dark to rescue a man, pulled him to safety, and employed artificial respiration to revive him. There were also times when other people failed to rescue a struggling, sinking swimmer, prompting Reagan to dive in, braving currents, to make the save. At Lowell Park he was more than just a champion swimmer—he was a lifesaver.

That fact should not be forgotten. On multiple occasions, Reagan plunged into treacherous waters, swam through dangerous currents, and pulled out helpless people at great personal risk. He saved lives. What must that have done for his psyche? Although later in life Reagan joked that most people he saved told him that they would have been fine without his help, he understood the importance of his job. Though he earned little money those summers, lifeguarding taught him the value of hard work and responsibility. And more important, it gave him a sense of self-worth. "You know why I had such fun at it?" he confessed. "Because I was the only one up there on the guard stand. It was like a stage. Everyone had to look up at me."

Beloved son, good student, football player, lifesaver—Dutch enjoyed riches that transcended dollars and cents. Added to his bounty were good

Swimming was Reagan's best sport. As a lifeguard at Lowell Park near Dixon, he saved seventy-seven floundering swimmers from drowning in the dangerous currents of the Rock River.

COLLEGE LIFE

It's hardly surprising that he had a girlfriend who seemed like she could have been cast in an Andy Hardy film. Margaret "Mugs" Cleaver, "a sparkling brunette," was the daughter of a minister of the Christian Church, the same congregation to which Dutch belonged. Their relationship was a charming high school one—not too serious, but serious enough to convince townspeople that the two would probably end up together in Dixon. Dutch, after all, seemed at home there, comfortable with its small-town pace. The motto below his picture in the high school yearbook, which read, "Life is just one grand sweet song, so start the music," suggested his ease with the direction of his life. If he had any excessive angst or ambition, it was invisible.

For the time being, Dutch Reagan was content to let Mugs lead the way. After her 1928 graduation, Mugs decided to attend tiny Eureka College, a Disciples of Christ institution less than one hundred miles south of Dixon. Dutch packed his steamer trunk into Mugs's car and went along. He had some money saved from another summer of lifeguarding, and once he reached Eureka, he worked out the other financial details for his admission, including a half-tuition athletic scholarship and a job washing dishes. It was enough, barely, to make ends meet.

He made the transition from Northside High School to Eureka College with an effortlessness that characterized the rest of his life. Eureka was small (only nine buildings and 187 students),

looks and a winning personality. By the time he was a senior in high school, he had sprouted to over six feet tall, and even at that young age he had matinee-idol looks. Always sociable, he starred in local dramatic productions, served as art editor for the Northside High School annual, and joined moral improvement groups. He wrote for the *Dixonian*, a student publication, and in his senior year was elected class president. All this good fortune he handled with an "aw-shucks" attitude.

coeducational, racially integrated, and church-centered. Its values were the ones his parents had always emphasized. And his good looks and ingratiating manners had always made him a welcome addition to any group, so with the ease of a lazy dive into the Rock River, Dutch became a college student.

The school and the student were well matched. Reagan was a young man of many talents, and Eureka needed students who went to class, played sports, and participated in extracurricular activities. "I fell head over heels in love with Eureka," he later admitted. And the affair was mutual.

Reagan thrived at Eureka, even if he did not excel in every aspect of college life. He pledged Tau

Kappa Epsilon, lived in the frat house, went out for the football team, and joined a host of organizations. He covered football games for the school paper, starred in dramatic productions, became the best performer on the swim team, edited the yearbook, and won elections for class and club offices.

He also contributed short stories to student literary collections. Most had themes drawn from his life. As biographer Edmund Morris noted, "Time and again in these stories, a tall, genial good-looking boy goes about his business (or lies comfortably doing nothing) untouched by and unconcerned by the agitation of others. He is sexy without being sexual, kind yet calculating, decent, dutiful, gentle,

In 1928, Reagan and his girlfriend Margaret Cleaver enrolled at Eureka College, a small school affiliated with the Disciples of Christ. Reagan (first row, fourth from right) played football, swam, and joined in a variety of other activities.

and massively self-centered." Also running through the stories is the "hero's intense delight at being looked at. The stare of any eyes . . . is as sensuous as the sun on his back."

Dutch was more active in the social, athletic, cultural, and political life of Eureka College than its academic one. He seemed to glide through his classes, passing but falling far short of distinction. His work ethic was unassailable. He didn't lack energy, drive, or ambition, but nevertheless floated through college without any concrete sense of direction.

His uncertainty paralleled the country's. The Midwest had been slogging through economic troubles when Dutch entered Eureka in September 1928, but by the fall of his sophomore year, matters had become decidedly worse. The October 1929 stock market crash began the steady slide toward the Great Depression, which lingered for more than a decade. A quarter of American workers lost their jobs. Many more saw their hours or wages slashed. In the Midwest, commodity prices tumbled, countless farmers lost their land, and the small towns that depended on agriculture suffered terribly.

Nestled in rural Illinois, Eureka College felt the sting of the times. Shortly after Dutch enrolled for the fall 1928 semester, Bert Wilson, the college's

Reagan (far right) was a standout on the undermanned swim team. He also helped to coach the squad.

The future president shows off his diving form while on the Eureka College swim team.

Reagan (top row, far right) continued his acting at Eureka College. He performed in a number of productions and even won recognition in a drama tournament at Northwestern University. He had the looks of a leading man.

Reagan was a starting guard on the Eureka football team. Although he had grown and put on weight, his coaches were more impressed by his work ethic than his athletic skills.

president, cut costs by eliminating some programs, combining others, and cutting faculty and staff positions. Although the board of trustees greenlighted the plan, most of the faculty and students opposed it. They demanded Wilson's resignation and the rejection of his draconian financial measures. But the board of trustees refused to yield and supported the president.

Reagan later recalled that around midnight on a Saturday in late November, just after the trustees voiced their opinion, the students organized a mass meeting to air their views. In his 1965 autobiography *Where's the Rest of Me?*, he described the mood of the gathering. In Reagan's account of the events, that afternoon Eureka had defeated Illinois College in a thrilling football game when Lump Watts made a field goal from more than fifty yards late in the fourth quarter. But the students in the stands hardly reacted to the play because they were consumed with talk of an impending strike and the newspaper reports of the college's plight.

Reagan claimed that he gave the decisive speech at that midnight meeting. After reviewing the history of the dispute, he moved passionately toward a call for a strike vote. As he studied the faces looking up at him, he realized that "an audience had a feel to it," and that he could move them toward his position. "When I came to actually presenting the motion there was no need for a parliamentary procedure: they came to their feet with a roar—even the faculty members present voted by acclamation. It was heady wine. Hell,

with two more lines I could have had them riding through 'every Middlesex village and farm'— without horses yet."

Dutch's discovery of his political voice is a wonderful story, marred only by a few factual errors: Illinois College drubbed Eureka 17–0, the game was on a Friday, the midnight assembly was on the Tuesday after the game, and newspaper reports of the gathering do not suggest that Reagan's speech was particularly important. As his telling of the episode illustrates, Reagan was capable of misremembering details in pursuit of a larger point and a better story.

The mundane details of Eureka's economic struggles were less important than Dutch's immersion into the currents of political action. After the conflict, he settled into Eureka's athletic and social scene. "As far as I am concerned," he told Eureka students in 1980, "everything good that has happened to me—everything—started here on this campus in those four years that still are such a part of my life."

Though he majored in sociology, Reagan took particular pride in his other achievements on campus. "I got poor marks . . . [but] I copped the lead in most plays. And in football I won three varsity sweaters." He graduated in the spring of 1932 with forty-four classmates, most of whom by this time were friends of his. Mugs also received her diploma. Soon after, Dutch and Mugs became engaged, as their friends and families expected. Now all he needed was a job and a career.

CHAPTER 2

THE ENTERTAINER

"I DIDN'T WANT TO HAVE A NET THROWN OVER ME. SECRETLY, I WAS CRAZY ABOUT ACTING."

—*RWR*

In June 1932, thousands of disenchanted World War I veterans descended on the nation's capital demanding early payment of cash bonuses they had been promised for their service. President Herbert Hoover, a cold and distant technocrat, never could muster the words needed to make Americans regain faith in their country. His platitudes about patience and self-reliance sounded more insensitive the farther the nation tumbled into its economic—and psychological—depression. The economy had been spiraling downward for nearly three years. Millions of Americans were unemployed, including Reagan's father.

When Dutch Reagan walked across the stage and received his sociology degree on that June day in 1932, he exchanged the comforting confines of Eureka College for a most uncertain world still reeling from the economic collapse of the Great Depression.

Ronald Reagan displays the easy charm and knockout smile that made him a hit with movie audiences.

His first summer after college closely resembled the ones of his recent past. He moved back into his parents' house, mounted his lifeguard's chair at Lowell Park, took Mugs on cheap dates, and pondered his next step. "I have no definite plans for the future outside of trying to get a position in some business, probably as a salesman," Reagan said. It made sense that he would instinctively chart a career that paralleled his father's. His academic performance at Eureka had been unspectacular. None of his classes had really grabbed him. He nursed a secret love for the stage, but acting seemed like an uncertain proposition at such a perilous time.

Unsure of his next move, Dutch took his dilemma to Sid Altschuler, a Kansas City businessman visiting town with his wife, a Dixon native. Dutch had a glancing relationship with Mr. Altschuler, having taught his two daughters how to swim. "What do you think you'd like to do?" Altschuler asked. "I don't know," Reagan admitted. He spent the next few days reminiscing about his triumphant career as a college thespian and his childhood performances with his mother. Finding Altschuler again, he confessed what he had long suppressed. "I want to be an actor," he said.

BEHIND THE MIC

Altschuler advised him to take any job he could find in the business. Heeding his advice, Dutch hitchhiked to Chicago only to encounter a series of closed doors. After returning to Dixon and lowering his sights a bit, he borrowed his father's car and drove seventy-five miles west to Davenport, Iowa, where he persuaded the manager of radio station WOC ("World of Chiropractic," a station housed in a chiropractic school) to give him a tryout. Reagan sat alone in a blue-curtained studio, calling an imaginary football game between Eureka College and Western State University. Eureka squeaked out a victory with some fictionalized, last-second heroics, and Reagan earned himself a probationary job.

Reagan announced some actual college football games for a few dollars apiece, and then waited by the phone to see whether WOC would offer a full-time post. Their call came in early 1933. Dutch Reagan, a twenty-two-year-old blessed with an engaging, distinctive baritone, would be WOC's

As a recent college graduate, Reagan had to carve out a career in the midst of the Great Depression.

newest staff announcer, earning an almost unbelievable one hundred dollars a month.

His innate optimism soared as he settled into his eighteen-dollar-a-month apartment in Davenport. The new president, Franklin D. Roosevelt, had promised Americans a New Deal. Reagan, who sported an FDR button throughout the 1932 campaign and cast his first-ever vote for the Democratic candidate, believed Roosevelt could turn the country around. Jack Reagan, who served as a county-level executive with two federal work-relief programs—the Civil Works Administration and the Works Progress Administration—certainly benefited from the New Deal.

It took a little time for Reagan to get acclimated behind the mic. He had a good voice but lacked technique. He struggled with reading spots cold, so he memorized them in advance and recited them from memory. Within weeks he became an important jack-of-all-trades at WOC. He read the news, introduced programs, spun records, and called the occasional sporting event.

After some initial struggles on the air, Reagan mastered the fluid, relaxed speaking style that served him well throughout his career.

Dutch was soon transferred to Des Moines, where he earned $200 per month as WHO's sports director. "Those were wonderful days," he recalled. WHO's 50,000-watt transmitter blasted his silky voice across the Midwest. On good nights it reached all the way to New Zealand. Boxers Jack Dempsey and Max Baer dropped by for interviews, as did actor Leslie Howard. Dutch became an able college football announcer, but his on-air reconstructions of Chicago Cubs games, which combined fragmentary telegraph reports with his own prodigious imagination, truly soared. Fans clustered around him whenever he reenacted games at the Iowa Fair Grounds. The story of him reporting that a batter fouled off pitch after pitch (a convenient way to fill dead air when his telegraph connection died) is an oft-told piece of Reagan lore. His daily sports commentaries and newspaper column, which often celebrated the morally uplifting qualities of sports, expanded his audience even further, and he became a popular speaker for local civic organizations.

Unlike most radio folk, Reagan's physical appearance garnered as much attention as his on-air skills. He had the looks of a leading man, not a disembodied radio announcer. Margaret Cleaver had recently mailed her engagement ring and a "Dear Dutch" letter from Europe. But this young, attractive, and affluent radio announcer brushed off the brush-off, at least publicly, and began an active dating life. "He is over six feet tall with the proverbial Greek-god physique: broad-shouldered, slim-waisted and a face that would make Venus look twice," gasped one local gossip columnist.

Reagan was already an actor in the sense that he was inventing a reality for his listeners. Still, he yearned for a bigger venue. Dutch's coworkers saw him as a modest, laid-back fellow, and he was. In what would become a recurring theme, they did not recognize the ambition beneath his complacent exterior.

In early 1936, Dutch convinced WHO to send him to Santa Catalina Island in California. So far as his bosses knew, he was gathering material for his re-creations by shadowing the Cubs throughout spring training. Dutch certainly did this, but he also seized the opportunity to try out for Hollywood. He had a slender cinematic connection in Joy Hodges, a former WHO employee who had made a few uncredited appearances in forgettable films. Hodges finagled a meeting with her agent, George Ward. "Just don't ever put those glasses on again," she advised after recoiling from Dutch's heavy, horn-rimmed spectacles.

Ward represented some bona fide stars, including Robert Taylor and Betty Grable. He also managed bit players such as Jane Wyman. After scrutinizing Reagan, Ward decided the young man might make a good "type" (a useful cog in some studio's machine) rather than a star, so he called Warner Bros., which agreed to schedule a screen test.

Reagan submitted to a battery of hairdressers, makeup artists, and lighting experts. A nervous wreck, he stood before the camera—at least, he assumed that dark blob was a camera—and recited the lines he had memorized over the weekend. And then it was over.

Dutch hopped a train back to Des Moines, thinking of the upcoming baseball season and assuming his Hollywood days had already ended. His hopes for making it in pictures were low when an unexpected telegram from Ward arrived. Dutch was shocked to discover that Warner Bros. was offering a nonbinding seven-year contract (which meant the studio could terminate him pretty much whenever it wanted) at $200 per week. "Sign before they change their minds," Reagan replied.

Reagan visiting East High School in Des Moines. His radio fame made him a popular guest at all kinds of public functions.

HOLLYWOOD

In May 1937, Reagan loaded up his brown Nash convertible for California. He made the 1,900-mile trip in three breakneck days, a remarkable feat in that pre-superhighway era (consider the old Hollywood movies in which wild car chases occur at only forty or fifty miles per hour).

Reagan (Warner Bros. insisted on calling him Ronald rather than Dutch) made the same journey that thousands of dispossessed Americans made during the Depression. Unlike the "Okies," to use the umbrella term referring to refugees from the Dust Bowl, Reagan journeyed to California feeling confident that a better—or at least more lucrative—future awaited him. If his long, bulky car roared past dissolute families and hobo jungles, he never mentioned them. At that point, he was only dimly aware of anything beyond his immediate circle. "There was a Spanish Civil War going on, the Japanese were again fighting in China, and Hitler repudiated the Versailles Treaty—but I wasn't mad at anyone," he later wrote. Worrying just wasn't in his nature. He was the kind of person who believed that the western sun he was driving into was actually rising on a wonderful new life in America's dream factory: Hollywood.

Reagan wasn't mad at anyone, but a lot of people in Hollywood were. The film community was in a touchy mood. Hollywood liberals were mobilizing against overseas tyranny, demanding a strong response to Hitler and Nazism. Employers and employees were also butting heads in a series of labor disagreements. Directors and screenwriters had formed unions after long struggles with the studios. Just two weeks before Reagan hit town, the studios finally recognized the Screen Actors Guild (SAG) following four years of antagonism and intense negotiations.

Reagan was too busy finding his way around the vast, heavily guarded Warner Bros. complex to ponder these developments—not that a more open schedule would have inspired much interest from the apolitical rookie. The studio really was a town unto itself. More precisely, it was exactly the kind of fabricated reality Reagan had crafted in his imaginary baseball games. Like those dramatic narratives spun from abbreviated telegrams, these Hollywood streets of apparently solid structures were actually false fronts buttressed by modest supports.

An awestruck Reagan wondered how he would fit into this glamorous new world. He dreamed of becoming an A-list Western star, a next-generation Tom Mix or William S. Hart—the kind of ten-gallon hero that John Wayne would become. More than anything, however, he wanted steady work. Warner Bros., like all the big studios, ground through talent at a relentless pace, micromanaging the images of actors who clicked and ditching those who didn't without a second thought.

Reagan found himself cast in a B movie called *Love Is on the Air* barely a week after he walked through the studio gates. This forgettable confection at least covered familiar territory, as he played a small-town radio announcer. His performance was convincing enough that Warner Bros. assigned him the lead in *Sergeant Murphy*, another B film. Sergeant Murphy, the title character, was a horse, making it the first but not last time that Reagan acted alongside an animal. The role let Reagan showcase his athleticism—he had recently been commissioned a second lieutenant in the U.S. Cavalry's Officers' Reserve Corps. His scenes with Murphy displayed an easy grace and quiet charm. Viewers could really believe that he loved a spirited beast that was too unruly for the military but had enough heart to win the prestigious Grand National in England.

In fact, Reagan seemed more at ease with the horse than with his human co-stars. His strengths and flaws asserted themselves throughout the nine films he made in 1938. He seemed uncomfortable in his own skin during such pictures as *Cowboy from Brooklyn*, *Girls on Probation*, and *Swing Your Lady*. Like many novice actors, he overemoted, relying on overly broad gestures and clamping a wide yet vague grin on his face whenever others were speaking in the scene. Reagan proved an expert at memorizing his lines, but when it came time to act, he recited rather than felt them, as if he were reading a recipe or an instruction manual. He emphasized saying the right words, not conveying the right emotions, and consistently began his line just a tad early, as if impatient for his conversation partner to finish.

At the same time, Reagan had undeniable charms. He had an engaging smile and looked

Reagan appeared in many B movies for Warner Bros. in the 1930s. Reagan's first movie, 1937's *Love Is on the Air*, let the rookie actor play a familiar role: a radio announcer.

Warner Bros. cast Reagan in a series of forgettable B movies such as *Girls on Probation* (1938), a formulaic crime picture co-starring Jane Bryan, who would later help convince Reagan to run for president.

good in a tuxedo. The studio's publicity material declared him "broad-shouldered and with a slender waistline . . . proficient in almost every sport." An exaggeration, to be sure, but one that captured the essence of his image. His smooth voice completed his charming, boy-next-door persona. He made a perfect sidekick or a nonthreatening best friend, the kind of upright guy you would ask to drive your best girl home.

The producers at Warner Bros. detected other assets. Reagan's desire for a steady paycheck outstripped his desire for A-list stardom. He never complained about the parts they gave him. He knew his lines, showed up on time, and always hit his marks. In the fast-paced, no-retakes world of B movies, Reagan became a pro's pro.

The studio rewarded his consistency with a secondary role in its high-budget prestige picture *Dark Victory* (1939). Intended as awards bait, *Dark Victory* was a turgid melodrama about society girl Judith Traherne—played by Bette Davis—and her fight against a malignant brain tumor. Humphrey Bogart, who wasn't *Humphrey Bogart* quite yet, played a rough but good-hearted Irish stable hand whose accent drifted in and out as the movie dragged on. Reagan was cast as Alec, a foppish, alcoholic playboy who in no way resembled the actor. Reagan would have begged off the project had he been a more demanding person.

"Was he in it?" Bette Davis replied when an interviewer inquired about Reagan's performance in the movie many years later. She could hardly be blamed, as Reagan had little to do except feign drunkenness. His character had no real purpose other than to invent reasons to exit the frame. Reagan's best moment came when Judith, deep in

her cups, rushes into a bar looking for more. "Here we go again," he sighs, in an unlikely foreshadowing of a more convincing performance he would give forty years later.

Dark Victory garnered more than its fair share of attention, but not enough to save Reagan from sinking back into B films. He had a soft landing, winning the part of fist-throwing Treasury agent Brass Bancroft in *Secret Service of the Air*, the first of four Brass Bancroft movies filmed between 1939 and 1940. The Bancroft films showed Reagan at his best. His natural physicality served him well as he

Reagan's performance as a drunken playboy in *Dark Victory* leaves Bette Davis looking unimpressed. This A-list film failed to elevate Reagan into the top ranks of Hollywood actors.

brawled with bad guys, crashed through windows, rode galloping horses, and dove from trains. The series had a tiny budget, which meant that Reagan performed many of his own stunts, although he retained a lifelong admiration for the professional stuntmen who did the really dangerous stuff.

Reagan remained a staunch Democrat. Despite his increasing political awareness, he appeared oblivious, or at least apathetic, to the fact that Warner Bros. used his Bancroft character as a tool for advancing President Roosevelt's foreign policy.

Hitler's September 1939 invasion of Poland ignited World War II in Europe. Asia had been in flames ever since Japan invaded China in 1937. Most Americans instinctively retreated into an isolationist shell. Roosevelt, however, urged heightened vigilance, a cautious military buildup, and a commitment to aiding democratic nations such as Great Britain and France. Hollywood executives, most of whom supported Roosevelt, started producing films that echoed the president's priorities. In 1939 Warner Bros. released both *Juarez*, a plodding biopic about Mexican revolutionary Benito Juarez that encouraged inter-American unity, and *Confessions of a Nazi Spy*, in which a determined FBI agent (played by Edward G. Robinson) smashes a German espionage operation.

Murder in the Air (1940), Reagan's final turn as Bancroft, was a political statement thinly disguised as a Saturday matinee. Bancroft had made his career from battling smugglers and counterfeiters. Now he took aim at an anti-American sabotage ring controlled by a decidedly Aryan band of evildoers. At stake is possession of an "inertia projector" that can blast enemy planes from the sky long before they breach America's borders. Bancroft wins the day, of course. With the projector in its hands, the United States became "invincible in war" and a mighty "force for world peace." Bancroft's triumph alerted viewers to the presence of foreign agitators while assuring them that a strong national defense offered the surest way of avoiding overseas entanglements.

A-LIST FILMS AND MARRIAGE

Reagan was no star, but he was getting regular work and sizable paychecks. He enjoyed the business of moviemaking and felt an almost childlike thrill at seeing himself projected on the silver screen. Life on the West Coast agreed with him, especially after he moved his parents to California. His brother, Neil, followed them, as did some Eureka College fraternity brothers. Warner Bros. hired Jack to read his son's fan mail, a sweetheart deal that Reagan deeply appreciated.

Los Angeles was Reagan's home now, but his family was not yet complete. He had dated many women (often for the studio's publicity purposes) since Margaret Cleaver had exited the scene. He showed little interest in long-term commitments, but a perky, snub-nosed blonde actress named Jane Wyman had other ideas.

Wyman had plugged her way through B movies since she was a teenager. The twenty-one-year-old

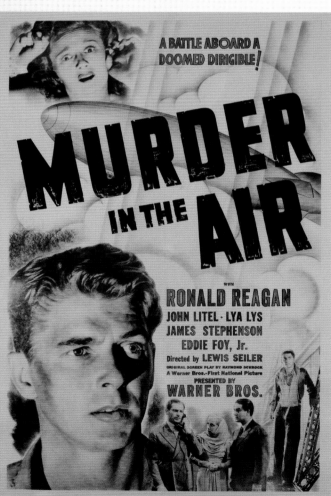

Brother Rat (1938) introduced Reagan to his future wife, actress Jane Wyman. At first he wasn't interested, but her smile in this publicity photo was genuine.

was unlucky in love, having just filed for her second divorce when she met Reagan in 1938 on the set of *Brother Rat*, a charming comedy about three high-spirited military cadets. She fell for him, and he for her, although he maintained a respectful distance so long as she remained legally married.

Studios typecast Wyman as a ditzy blonde. She was actually an intelligent, sensitive woman prone to worrying and mood swings. Perhaps it was Reagan's calm solidity that appealed to her. "He was such a sunny person," she remembered. They began dating.

A moment in *Brother Rat and a Baby* (1940), *Brother Rat*'s entertaining sequel, perfectly captured each partner's role in their romance. Wyman, playing the none-too-bright but cute-as-a-button daughter of Reagan's old commanding officer, wobbles arm-in-arm with Reagan after drinking a bit too much champagne ("ginger ale with some music in it," she calls it). She leans in for a kiss. He demurs before finally giving in. She keeps leaning. Wyman is the pursuer. Reagan merely reacts to her desire.

Their courtship had an avid supporter in Louella Parsons, a powerful Hollywood gossip columnist. Reagan had first met Parsons on the set of *Hollywood Hotel* (1937). She happened to hail from Dixon and, like pretty much everyone else, found Reagan affable and charming. She began promoting his career in her column, and later promoted the Reagan-Wyman team, calling them "two of Hollywood's nicest people." When the actors wed in 1940, Parsons hosted a reception at her home.

Just a week before his wedding, Reagan read a *Variety* notice announcing that Warner Bros. was preparing to shoot a biopic about Knute Rockne, the famous Notre Dame football coach. Reagan's friend Pat O'Brien, his co-star from *Cowboy from Brooklyn*, was set for the title role.

Reagan, who never fought for parts, really wanted to be in that picture. He had long revered the legendary halfback George Gipp, the inspiration for Rockne's stirring and almost certainly fictional "win one for the Gipper" halftime speech. Gipp offered the kind of rousing sports story that Reagan loved writing about back in his Iowa days. At Reagan's behest, O'Brien lobbied studio chief Jack Warner for a chance at the part. "Who's the Gipper?" a clueless Warner asked. O'Brien trumpeted Reagan's qualifications until Warner Bros. agreed to screen-test the half-blind former lineman. Reagan won the role, along with a future nickname.

Even though his part occupies only fifteen minutes of *Knute Rockne, All American* (1940), Reagan's Gipp is the heart and soul of the film. "What's your name?" Rockne asks after watching

as the athletic young stranger kicks a football into the stratosphere. "Gipp, George Gipp," he snaps. "What's yours?"

Reagan nails Gipp's transformation from sullen, smart-mouthed kid to reluctant media star. "I don't like people to get too close to me," he says in a line more revealing of the actor than the character he portrayed. Reagan still rushes through his lines, but he gives a lovely "win one for the Gipper" deathbed speech. "I had a lump in my throat so big I couldn't talk," he wrote in his autobiography.

Knute Rockne led to Reagan getting cast as General George Custer, alongside Errol Flynn's Jeb Stuart in *Santa Fe Trail* (1940). Two more A films (low-budget As, or what Reagan called "shaky As"), *The Bad Man* and *International Squadron* (1941), followed.

NOTABLE FILMS

1937
Love Is on the Air

1938
Swing Your Lady
Sergeant Murphy
Accidents Will Happen
Cowboy from Brooklyn
Boy Meets Girl
Girls on Probation
Brother Rat
Going Places

1939
Secret Service of the Air
Dark Victory
Code of the Secret Service
Naughty but Nice
Hell's Kitchen
The Angels Wash Their Faces
Smashing the Money Ring

Reagan usually let film roles come to him, but he had dreamed of playing George Gipp for years. His believable pose as a football player suggests that Warner Bros. selected the right man for the part.

As Reagan's star was rising, the world plunged deeper into war. Within five years of leaving Iowa, he had reached the top of the second tier of Hollywood actors. He was no James Cagney or Clark Gable, but audiences at least recognized him. At Jane's encouragement, he joined the Screen Actors Guild, an organization destined to raise his public profile even higher. His personal life was thriving, and he had recently become a father. Daughter Maureen Reagan was born in January 1941. The only sour note that year came when Jack Reagan, whose drifting and alcoholism profoundly affected his son, died that May.

During that time, the good outweighed the bad for Reagan. He and Jane had a new agent, MCA's Lew Wasserman, who negotiated contracts that would pay them the princely sum of $750,000 over the next several years. Their financial security ensured, the Reagans built a home in the hills overlooking Sunset Boulevard. From there, Reagan prepared for a challenging part in what would become his most critically acclaimed film: *Kings Row*.

Reagan was just breaking into A-list films when he co-starred with Olivia de Havilland and notorious scene-stealer Errol Flynn in *Santa Fe Trail* (1940). Unfortunately, Flynn's performance as future Confederate general Jeb Stuart was about as convincing as Reagan's George Custer.

CHAPTER 3

FIGHTING WORLD WAR II AT FORT ROACH

"WITH WEEKS OF SHOOTING ON *DESPERATE JOURNEY* STILL REMAINING, I RECEIVED A LETTER THAT DIDN'T EVEN NEED OPENING: ON THE OUTSIDE, STAMPED IN RED, WERE THE WORDS, 'IMMEDIATE ACTION ACTIVE DUTY.'"

—*RWR*

Americans were divided, jittery about the future. In September 1939, the armies of German dictator Adolf Hitler had fired the first shots in the European phase of World War II when they marched into Poland. In the spring of 1940, Germany invaded and defeated Denmark, Norway, Belgium, Luxembourg, the Netherlands, and France, before turning its attention to Great Britain. Hitler's blitzkrieg prompted a vigorous debate between Americans who wanted to aid Britain in the conflict and others who argued that the United States should not become involved in the war.

War came for America at the same time that Ronald Reagan was blossoming into a Hollywood star. But like millions of other Americans, he wore the uniform of his country and performed his military duties to the best of his ability.

More than 800,000 people paid for memberships in the America First Committee, which opposed any action that would entangle the United States in the European or Asian wars. Organized at Yale, its members included future president Gerald Ford, future Peace Corps director Sargent Shriver, and future U.S. Supreme Court justice Potter Stewart. But the best-known member of the organization was famed aviator Charles Lindbergh. He crisscrossed the country giving speeches against American involvement in the war and criticizing those who fueled the interventionist impulse.

MOVIES WITH MESSAGES

High on Lindbergh's list of culprits were members of the motion picture industry. Lindbergh and noninterventionists in Congress contended that such films as *Blockade* (1938), *Confessions of a Nazi Spy* (1939), *Foreign Correspondent* (1940), *The Great Dictator* (1940), and *Sergeant York* (1941) were mustering support for intervention and marching America toward war. As Senator Gerald P. Nye charged, Americans watched movies to be entertained, but in the darkness of the theaters, Hollywood producers and writers were slipping

In *Murder in the Air* (1940), one of four Brass Bancroft films, Reagan played a part—albeit a small one—in preparing America for war. In the film, Brass alerts viewers to the growing fascist espionage threat.

Reagan with Olympe Bradna in *International Squadron* (1941). Reagan portrays a wisecracking American who joins the Royal Air Force and learns the meaning of valor and sacrifice. Like many World War II action films, it criticizes individualism and centers on the importance of the group in combat.

them an interventionist message. "Before you know where you are, you have actually listened to a speech designed to make you believe that Hitler is going to get you," Nye claimed.

By 1940, Warner Bros., Ronald Reagan's home studio, led the Hollywood call for intervention. Jack Warner, head of production for the studio, told a congressional committee investigating the film industry that he believed that Nazism was "an evil force," and that he supported aid to Great Britain. He was proud of the messages in *Confessions of a Nazi Spy* and *Sergeant York*. He was similarly

pleased with the low-budget message films that featured Ronald Reagan, such as *Murder in the Air* and *International Squadron*, in which Reagan portrays an American pilot flying for the Royal Air Force who gives his life in defense of Britain. As the star of both films, Reagan became associated in the public's mind with the heroic defense of America and its ideals.

As the United States edged closer to intervention, and concerns about Americans fighting overseas increased, Hollywood registered the nation's mood. A few producers made disquieting films

Reagan and Robert Cummings in *Kings Row* (1942). The film was a blockbuster Hollywood melodrama and a breakout role for the young actor. Based on a sensational novel by Henry Bellamann, some insiders doubted the film would ever make it past the censors, but screenwriter Casey Robinson scrubbed the script until it was just presentable enough to make it to the screen.

that called into question stock types. In Alfred Hitchcock's *Shadow of a Doubt* (1943), the charming, wisecracking Uncle Charlie, played by Joseph Cotton, is revealed as a dark, troubled murderer. Even more disturbing was Ronald Reagan's most critically acclaimed film, producer Hal B. Wallis's *Kings Row* (1942). Directed by Sam Wood and starring Ann Sheridan, Robert Cummings, and Reagan, it populates a typical American small town with a sadistic doctor, a thieving banker, a nymphomaniac, and several other characters deranged enough to make censors nervous.

Although screenwriters and censors cut several of the most disturbing scenes from Henry Bellamann's sensational novel, enough remained in the film to shock moviegoers. The worst involved Drake McHugh (Reagan), the easygoing sidekick of the terminally earnest Parris Mitchell (Cummings). The film presents Drake as a charming, spoiled, rich kid, something of a ladies' man, but basically harmless and hardly a libertine. He certainly does not deserve the fate the script deals him. First a scoundrel banker absconds with his trust fund, leaving him penniless. Then, after he is involved in

THUMBS UP! HEARTS UP! HEADS UP!

INTERNATIONAL SQUADRON

THEIR COMRADES CONQUERED...THEIR COURAGE UNCONQUERED!

RONALD REAGAN

OLYMPE BRADNA · WILLIAM LUNDIGAN · JOAN PERRY · REGINALD DENNY

Directed by LEWIS SEILER · Presented by WARNER BROS.

She's a good girl FOR GUYS TO LET ALONE!

SHERIDAN · REAGAN

Juke Girl

ANN SHERIDAN · ROBERT CUMMINGS · RONALD REAGAN · BETTY FIELD

Presented by WARNER BROS. Pictures Inc.

KINGS ROW

Ann Sheridan and Robert Cummings confront the invalid Reagan, hoping that the truth might give him the will to live a full life. Reagan considered *Kings Row* to be his finest work.

Drake McHugh (Reagan) and Randy Monaghan (Ann Sheridan) play the most dramatic scene in *Kings Row*. "Randy, where's the rest of me?" Drake asks, his voice filled with horror.

a minor railroad accident, a criminally judgmental, sadistic surgeon amputates his legs at the hips. The moment when Drake awakens after the operation is the dramatic apex of Reagan's acting career.

The scene was "rough to play," recalled Reagan, because in a few seconds he had to move "from unconsciousness to full realization" of his loss. "Worst of all, I had to give my reaction in a line of no more than five words."

Reagan knew he had "neither the experience nor the talent to fake it." He "rehearsed the scene before mirrors, in corners of the studio, while driving home, in the men's rooms at restaurants, before selected friends." He consulted physicians and psychologists, amputees and disabled people. "I got a lot of answers." But none equipped him to capture that terrible moment. By the day of the shooting he was racked with panic.

His actual worry, frustration, sleeplessness, and fear of failure helped prepare him for the scene. He appeared on the sound stage looking wan and helpless. He wandered over to review the set. Beneath the quilt, which would cover most of his body in the scene, the prop man had cut a hole in the mattress. Reagan climbed into the rig and waited almost an hour, "contemplating my torso and the smooth undisturbed flat of the covers where my legs should have been."

The totality of the moment—his fear of failure, the discomfort of the rigging, the depth of the scene—terrified him. Then he heard Sam Wood speak in a low voice. "Do you want to shoot it?"

"No rehearsal," Reagan answered.

"Let's make it," Wood ordered. "Action!"

Drake McHugh awakes in a modest workman's bedroom close to the train tracks. His eyes come to life, glancing toward the bottom of the bed. Simple fear gives way to abject terror. He instinctively calls to his love interest Randy Monaghan (Ann Sheridan). "Randy! Randy!" he screams. She bursts into the room. (Actually, Sheridan was not in the camera shot for the crucial line, so she was not required to be in the room. But, Reagan wrote, "she knew it was one of those scenes where a fellow actor needed all the help he could get and at that moment, in my mind, she was Randy answering my call.")

With the camera centered on a tight chest and head shot, Drake, panic and fear in his eyes, cries, "Randy! Where's the rest of me?"

There was no need for another take. He caught the moment perfectly on the first take. "Perhaps I never did quite as well again in a single shot," he wrote.

Kings Row was the sort of film that Hollywood did exceedingly well—melodrama with a message,

sensationalism with a moral. The world was a bad place full of evil people, it suggested, but in the end good can triumph and happiness can prevail. Reagan's role was intended to attract attention and positive press.

A CAREER INTERRUPTED

During the previous few years, Warner Bros. had strategically advanced Reagan's movie persona with heroic adventure roles and light comedies. They cast him in supporting roles and did not force him to carry an important picture.

By the beginning of 1942, their strategy was beginning to pay dividends. A January 1942 Gallup survey ranked him 74th (tied with Laurence Olivier) in a list of the top 100 stars. He was especially popular with younger theatergoers. One in ten people polled said they would go to a movie just to see Reagan. And that was before the release of *Kings Row*. "Reagan has never appeared to such excellent advantage," commented a *New Yorker* reviewer. On the basis of his performance and his potential, agent Lew Wasserman negotiated a new contract for the actor, with a weekly salary that began at $1,650 and escalated to $5,000. The making of stars was a fickle business in Hollywood; it was never a science. But by this time, Reagan had nearly climbed to the top. He was now ready to star in big-budget features.

Shortly thereafter, world events disrupted the plans Warner Bros. had for Reagan. On December 7, 1941, the Japanese ended the intervention debate and bombed Pearl Harbor, sending the United States into war. The next day, thousands of Americans enlisted, and the Selective Service board geared up to draft millions more. Despite the fact that in 1942, Colonel Lewis B. Hershey, the director of the Selective Service, designated the film industry as critical "to the national health, safety and interest, and in other instances to war production"—effectively putting it on equal footing with farming and steel production—the onset of the war changed how Hollywood did business.

War changed the business, but it didn't end the business. The industry continued to make films and profits, supporting the country's war efforts and enriching the studio heads. But the war made Hollywood leading men an endangered species. Leading men, especially action heroes like Ronald Reagan, projected strength, virility, and bravery. They personified exactly what Americans expected from their soldiers and sailors. Therefore, if they were not in uniform, Americans were apt to ask, "Why not?"

In the days and months after the start of the war, many of Hollywood's most-revered male stars patted their horses, kissed their wives, and traded in their civvies for uniforms. Henry Fonda enlisted in the Navy, Clark Gable in the Army, Tyrone Power in the Marines, and Jimmy Stewart in the Army Air Corps. David Niven and Laurence

Even during the war, many things remained the same in Hollywood. Actors acted, directors directed, pictures got made, and premieres took place. Lieutenant Ronald Reagan and his wife Jane Wyman attend the premiere of *Thirty Seconds Over Tokyo*, MGM's 1944 film based on the 1942 Doolittle raid.

Olivier returned to England to enlist; Sterling Hayden, Burgess Meredith, Gilbert Roland, and other actors also answered America's call for service. So did directors John Ford, William Wyler, John Huston, and Frank Capra; producers Jack Warner, Hal Roach, and Darryl F. Zanuck; writer Garson Kanin; and cameraman Gregg Toland. Thousands of Hollywood personnel went into service, as did professional baseball players and boxers, and more than sixteen million other Americans.

Although Reagan was already a reserve cavalry officer, Warner Bros. maneuvered to prevent him from being called up for active duty. In 1941 and 1942, the studio applied for and received three deferments for him, allowing him to finish work on *Kings Row*, *Juke Girl*, and *Desperate Journey*. Finally on April 14, 1942, just a few days after Japan defeated American forces on the Bataan Peninsula, and a few days before the heroic Doolittle raid, Reagan went on active duty and was assigned to Fort Mason in San Francisco.

Before they lost him to the service, Warner Bros. squeezed a few more feature films from their emerging star. In *Juke Girl*, Reagan teamed up again with Ann Sheridan in a movie that was singularly poorly timed. It was larded with Great Depression and New Deal concerns. Based on a *Saturday Evening Post* exposé of rural poverty, it centers on a conflict between itinerant crop pickers and wealthy shippers. Reagan was cast as Steve Talbot, a handsome, heavy-hitting picker who takes on a ruthless, greedy shipper and wins. Along the

way, he also captures the heart of a cynical juke girl (Sheridan). *Juke Girl* falls short of its mark as a social film, and falls short as a screwball comedy as well, ending up as some sort of strange fusion of *The Grapes of Wrath* and *They Drive by Night,* with a little romance thrown in for good measure.

Yet even if the movie had been good—which it wasn't—it would have still been the wrong film for America in 1942. As President Franklin Roosevelt knew, "Dr. New Deal" had been replaced by "Dr. Win the War." The government wanted Hollywood to produce movies that would help to aid the war effort. That, after all, was why the Roosevelt administration was willing to give deferments to workers in the film industry and to allow the studio heads to continue to rake in profits.

HOLLYWOOD GOES TO WAR

What specifically did Washington, D.C., expect from Hollywood? First, the Office of War Information (OWI) thought that the motion picture industry could explain the issues in the war to everyday Americans. In the months after Pearl Harbor, only 13 percent of Americans could name one of Roosevelt's Four Freedoms, and a mere 5 percent could give an ideological reason for the conflict. For millions of Americans, Pearl Harbor was seen as the only cause of the war, and the nature of their country's conflict with Germany and Italy was as nebulous as the fine print on a legal document. It was the job of filmmakers like Frank Capra, the driving force behind the seven-part Why We Fight series, to give the American people an entertaining crash course in geopolitics.

Second, the OWI, working through its Hollywood arm, the Bureau of Motion Pictures (BMP), wanted movies that delivered messages about America's allies and enemies, as well as the battles to be won on both the battlefield and the home front. The *Government Information Manual for the Motion Picture Industry*, the BMP's guidebook for Hollywood, asked that every film project begin with a simple question: "Will this picture help win the war?" With that object in mind, filmmakers were told to present an image of a unified America—undivided by any class, religious, ethnic, gender, racial, or labor cleavages—populated by happy, busy, productive, and patriotic citizens who obey rationing laws, give up their seats on public transportation to servicemen, plant Victory Gardens, and make countless other small sacrifices to help win the war.

The BMP also reviewed scripts and finished films to make certain that America's allies were scrubbed and sparkling. For example, in *Mrs. Miniver* (1942), the British class system was all but

Flynn and Reagan had to put the mission—and the war—above their desires for heroism and fun. The film unwittingly suggests that, left uninterrupted, the nasty Germans would probably have wiped themselves out.

erased; in *Mission to Moscow* (1943), communism was made to look like capitalism with a social conscience, and Joe Stalin was warm and avuncular; and in *China* (1943), the army of Chiang Kai-shek fights with efficiency and bravery. In Hollywood's version of World War II, America's allies were selfless and loyal, just as its Japanese and Nazi enemies were cruel and cunning.

In the context of these changes in Hollywood, Reagan made one World War II film before he was called up. Starring the swashbuckling Errol Flynn as Flight Lieutenant Terrence Forbes and cocksure Ronald Reagan as Flying Officer Johnny Hammond, *Desperate Journey* (1942) attempted to please both the BMP and the viewers, who expected Flynn to engage in some foolish, life-threatening mission every ten minutes or so, as he had done in previous films. The film had Alan Hale for slapstick, and Arthur Kennedy, who delivered the BMP's earnest message about the importance of the mission over individual gratification or glory. Reagan's job was to look handsome, smile, wisecrack, and volunteer for suicide missions. More than anything, *Desperate Journey* underscored the tensions between the political goals of the BMP and the we-know-our-audience approach of Hollywood producers.

Particularly sloppy was the film's treatment of Germans. The studio wanted to satisfy the BMP's notion that all Nazis were irredeemably evil, while somehow maintaining the idea that not all Germans were bad (after all, millions of

Ronald Reagan played a cocky Brooklyn pilot in *Desperate Journey* (1942).

Americans had German ancestry). Raymond Massey, the Oxford-educated actor who had portrayed Abraham Lincoln in *Abe Lincoln in Illinois* (1940), plays Nazi Major Otto Baumeister with a ruthless, inconsiderate gusto that he directs at his subordinates as well as his enemies. He gives the impression that, if left alone, Nazis would happily eliminate each other. In contrast, Nancy Coleman plays an anti-Nazi German with such sweetness and conviction that viewers probably wondered how such good people came to be led by such bad men.

For Reagan, *Desperate Journey* was a final nod to the industry he had grown to love. The same poor eyesight that hampered him on the football field made him a poor candidate for any activity that involved shooting, so there was never a chance that he would be shipped to a combat zone after basic training. After a battery of tests, the army classified him as eligible only for "limited service."

RONALD REAGAN'S WAR

Fittingly, he was assigned to a job that ideally suited his skill set—acting, communicating, and making movies. After just over a month in San Francisco, Reagan returned to Los Angeles to join Lieutenant Colonel Jack Warner's First Motion Picture Unit (FMPU). The unit was the brainchild of General Henry H. "Hap" Arnold, commander of the Army Air Corps. Intelligent, forward-looking, and devoted to the corps, Arnold created the FMPU in 1942 after prolonged discussions with Warner. The unit's job was to make films that promoted the strategic benefits of air power, aided recruitment, helped train pilots, and improved service morale, unity, and efficiency.

At this time, the U.S. Army and Navy were buzzing with activity and growth, but the Air Corps was just coming into its own during the early years of the war. In 1938 the Air Corps had fewer than 22,000 men and 3,900 planes. By the end of 1944, the Air Corps had more than 2.5 million men, and American factories were producing 145,000 planes a year. It was on its way to becoming an independent branch of the armed forces. During these

In real life, recently promoted Captain Ronald Reagan was assigned to the Army Air Corps' First Motion Picture Unit (FMPU), where he helped produce training and propaganda films. While his duties did not involve combat, they did call for service to his country.

years of growth, Reagan and the FMPU labored to give the corps a face and a voice, distinguishing its mission and achievements for itself as much as for other Americans. This was an important and difficult task, and Reagan excelled in his role in it.

Initially, the FMPU was housed at Warner Bros.' Vitagraph Studios in Los Angeles. It quickly outgrew the facility and in October 1942 was relocated to Hal Roach Studios in Culver City. Members of the unit often referred to their duty base as Fort Roach. Others called it Fort Wacky, but far more work than antics took place on the post.

During his brief time in Hollywood, Reagan had starred in several films that cast him as an aviator hero, including *Secret Service of the Air*, *Murder in the Air*, *International Squadron*, and *Desperate Journey*. Ironically, he hated to fly. But that hardly mattered to Hollywood producers or the FMPU's filmmakers. Reagan looked like what they thought a pilot should look like (hometown-boy handsome) and projected the cool sangfroid that pilots should project. This made him perfect to appear in or narrate the FMPU's recruitment films.

All aspects of flight combat were dangerous, but the position of rear gunner in a bomber was especially so. The film *Rear Gunner* (1943) was made to be shown in commercial theaters to boost enlistment by presenting the rear gunner as a "modern knight of fire." Starring Burgess Meredith as a "timid farm hand" from Kansas, the film follows him from his selection as a potential gunner by an observant lieutenant (Reagan), through gunnery

One of the FMPU's films was *Recognition of the Japanese Zero Fighter* (1943). Reagan was cast as a P-40 pilot who mistakes an American plane for the enemy. The film reinforced how crucial it was for pilots to instantly identify warplanes.

training, and into combat, where his valiant actions are rewarded with the Distinguished Service Medal. The job of rear gunner, an instructor tells the farm boy, is important. The leaders of the corps "know that the fire from your guns is the fire of freedom."

Although Reagan appeared in several early FMPU films, by 1943 the unit had begun to cast more nonprofessionals on camera, using Reagan as the narrator. His voice was calm and persuasive, mixing warmth, humor, and charm in just the right amounts. His accent had a Middle America, boy-next-door sound. He projected Mr. Average, and fan magazines reinforced the image. In one he wrote, "I like to swim, hike and sleep (eight hours a night). I'm fairly good at every sport except tennis, which I don't like. My favorite menu is steak smothered in onions and strawberry shortcake. Mr. Norm is my alias . . . Nothing about me to make me stand out on the midway."

It was that Jimmy Stewart/Gary Cooper ability *not* to stand out that made him such a standout. In the Academy Award–winning *Beyond the Line of Duty* (1942), Reagan narrated the story of Captain Hewitt T. Wheless, a flier who won the

Distinguished Service Cross and was mentioned by President Roosevelt in one of his famous Fireside Chats. The film featured the voices of both Reagan and Roosevelt, combining two of the finest communicators in Washington and Hollywood.

Reagan's effectiveness and star power won him a major role in *This Is the Army* (1943), Hollywood's all-star tribute to America's men and women in uniform. Based on Irving Berlin's 1942 Broadway hit that raised millions of dollars for the Army

Reagan, with Frances Langford, was chosen for a lead role in the Warner Bros. hit *This Is the Army* (1943), which was based on Irving Berlin's Broadway musical and raised funds for the Army Emergency Relief.

Emergency Relief, the movie was an elaborate song-and-dance production that featured Reagan as the author of the show.

Reagan met Berlin several times during the filming. In one scene, the fabled songwriter was so impressed with the actor that, according to Reagan, Berlin suggested, "You really should give this business some consideration when the war is over. It's very possible that you could have a career in show business." The comment made Dutch wonder if Berlin had actually seen any of his films, or if the war had been going on so long that Reagan had already been forgotten.

Many of his khaki-clad colleagues were wondering the same thing. The war made and ended careers. When it began, John Wayne was not yet

Reagan with his mother, Nelle. The two were devoted to each other. Reagan's father, Jack, died on May 18, 1941.

an established star. He had been working in the industry for more than a decade, and in 1941 had just begun to get leading roles at major studios. During the conflict, Wayne had received a series of deferments, starred in a dozen features, and become a star. During Reagan's three years in uniform, he had appeared in only one commercial film (*Desperate Journey*), and even then in an undistinguished role.

On September 10, 1945, just a week after Japan signed an official surrender, Reagan's active duty ended and he returned to civilian life. Would moviegoers who had been introduced to other stars still be interested in him? It was a question that troubled his thoughts.

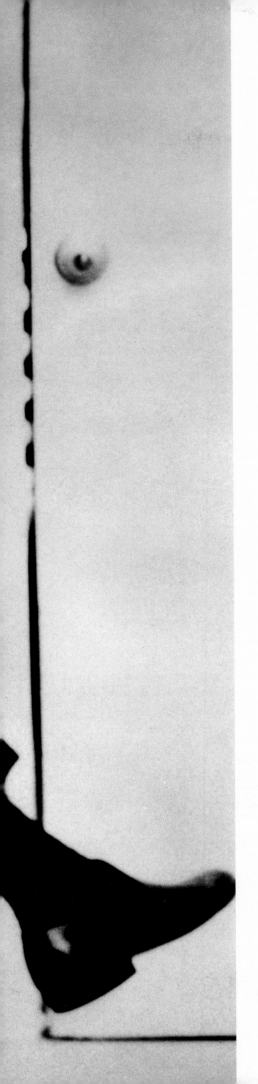

CHAPTER 4

A LIFE REINVENTED

"TRUE, I'D BEEN MAKING HANDSOME MONEY EVER
SINCE WORLD WAR II, BUT THAT HANDSOME MONEY
LOST A LOT OF ITS BEAUTY AND SUBSTANCE GOING
THROUGH THE 91 PERCENT TAX BRACKET."

—*RWR*

O n V-J Day in the summer of 1945, as his days in uniform ended, Ronald Reagan still had no lofty ambitions.
"By the time I got out of the Army Air Corps," he later wrote,
"all I wanted to do—in common with several million other
veterans—was to rest up for awhile, make love to my wife, and
come up refreshed to a better job in an ideal world." He added
parenthetically, "As it came out, I was disappointed in all these
postwar ambitions."

Until that point he had lived a charmed existence. He had
moved from one stage in his life to the next in classic "pluck and
luck" fashion. To be sure, he worked hard and made the most of
his opportunities, but at every step he had been blessed with the

After the end of World War II, Reagan returned to Warner Bros. and
resumed his career. But he was no longer a rising young actor, and
he did not land big roles. Eventually he turned to television, where
he was the host of *General Electric Theater*.

As Reagan's career stalled, Jane Wyman's took off. She received acclaim for her performances in *The Lost Weekend* (1945), *The Yearling* (1947), and *Johnny Belinda* (1948). The couple's work schedules put a strain on their marriage.

good fortune of being in the right place at the right time. Then, toward the end of 1945, when he was thirty-four years old, the life he had built began to crumble. His marriage to Jane Wyman ended, his acting career hit a crisis stage, and his political beliefs faced challenges. With everything he thought was stable now falling apart, Reagan might have felt sorry for himself and given up. But he didn't. The struggles caused him to reexamine his life and beliefs, prompting changes in every aspect. Without losing the best of himself, over the next twenty years Reagan discovered the rest of himself.

LOVE LOST AND FOUND

Hollywood marriages between ambitious actors have always been high-risk mergers. Keeping a marriage alive and vital is a herculean task in an occupation that is emotionally demanding and often requires long hours at work, significant travel, time away from home, and intense associations with others. Ronald Reagan and Jane Wyman's marriage looked fairy-tale perfect from the outside—indeed, such columnists as Louella Parsons and Hedda Hopper made it appear so—but by the end of the war, problems had surfaced.

Wyman was a talented, intelligent professional, dedicated to her craft and frustrated with the direction of her career at Warner Bros. For a decade, studio producers had cast her as the stereotypical ditzy blonde in low-budget comedies and had refused her entreaties for more serious roles. Toward the end of the war, she won the right to work for other studios and, as a result, her career shot upward. Wyman garnered critical acclaim for her role as the wife of an alcoholic in Billy Wilder's *The Lost Weekend* (1945), received an Academy Award nomination for Best Actress for *The Yearling* (1947), and won the Best Actress Oscar for her performance as a deaf-mute in *Johnny Belinda* (1948). In a little more than three years, she had finally achieved stardom.

But her fame came with a price. Far more than her husband, Wyman lost herself in her roles. After long days on the set playing lonely, unhappy, and unfulfilled characters, she often had trouble resuming her "real" life. Reagan understood this, and gave her the emotional space she needed while he worked to resurrect his own career. Despite these efforts, there was no denying that their marriage suffered.

The arrival of children did not help. Wyman gave birth to Maureen Elizabeth in 1941, just before her husband went into the army, and the couple adopted Michael Edward in 1945, shortly before Reagan returned home. On June 26, 1947, Wyman and Reagan had a third and final child, a daughter named Christine, who died a day later. At that time, Reagan was seriously ill with viral pneumonia. Unfortunately, Reagan and Wyman

To the outside world, the Reagans—Ron and Jane, Maureen and Michael—presented a portrait of a happy Hollywood family. But in 1949, they divorced.

faced their respective medical crises alone, unable to properly support one another.

After these ongoing struggles, the marriage did not last much longer. Wyman filed for divorce in February 1948, citing as grounds "extreme mental cruelty." That charge, however, simply fulfilled the legal requirements of the state. Reagan had never been intentionally cruel, and his daughter later wrote that he was "devastated" by Wyman's decision. He believed that marriages were binding moral contracts, not something to flee at the first sign of trouble.

Wyman told the court that the two had grown apart. Her husband was more interested in his political work in the Screen Actors Guild than he was in her career, she said, and "there was nothing in common between us, nothing to sustain our marriage." The divorce became final in July 1949.

The end of his marriage, Reagan admitted later, left him feeling empty inside. Yet he was not the sort of person to be crushed by failure or to dwell on the past. He still had family, career, and political concerns that demanded his energies, so he did what he had done all his life—adjusted to his new circumstances and got on with the business of living.

That meant spending time with his children—reading stories to Maureen and Michael when they were small, and teaching them to swim and ride as they got older. He also continued his film career and SAG interests unabated, never permitting his sense of rejection to interfere with his work.

Soon he even began dating other women. Sometimes the outings were dinners with co-stars, the kind of occasions arranged by the studio to publicize his latest film. He spent several evenings with Patricia Neal, his co-star in *The Hasty Heart* (1950), but she sensed that he was still pining for Jane Wyman.

In the fall of 1949, he enjoyed an arranged dinner date with Nancy Davis, a competent working actress who did not share the same unwavering ambition as Wyman. Raised in comfortable surroundings in Chicago, Davis had graduated from

Smith College with majors in English and drama. In the mid-1940s, she appeared in several Broadway plays before receiving a screen test and signing a seven-year contract with Metro-Goldwyn-Mayer Studios. MGM almost immediately began to cast her in "dependable women" roles—faithful wife, loyal friend, reliable mother.

Her film work elicited encouraging reviews, but it was apparent to her friends that she wanted something more lasting and emotionally rewarding than a movie career. In the biographical information she gave to MGM, she confessed that her "greatest ambition" was to enjoy "a successful happy marriage." Some writers have suggested that she was

After his divorce from Jane Wyman, Reagan was cautious about relationships. But in Nancy Davis he found an ideal match. She was a working actress who dreamed about a happy marriage more than an Oscar.

After a lengthy courtship, Ronald Reagan and Nancy Davis married. They enjoyed a loving marriage and eventually formed a successful political team.

desperate for a husband, which was far from the truth. She was, however, ready for marriage with a steady, loving, thoughtful man. Ronald Reagan seemed typecast for the role.

Soon Reagan and Davis became an item in the insular Hollywood community. They often had dinner at Chasen's, a restaurant near Beverly Hills popular with Reagan, Jimmy Stewart, Frank Sinatra, and other A-list stars. They spent quiet evenings with friends and relaxed during uneventful weekends at a favorite spot on the Pacific Coast. Reagan did not rush the relationship. He was not about to jump into another marriage.

After almost three years of dating, of talking about life, ambitions, and politics, Reagan finally proposed to Nancy at his favorite booth at Chasen's.

After their wedding on March 4, 1952, the newlyweds cut their wedding cake at a party in the home of actor William Holden.

They were married on March 4, 1952. More than just an ideal couple, they were a good team. They shared values, interests, and goals, and complemented one another. He was social and easy to work with, and she had a knack for evaluating people. Jane Wyman had been bored by politics; Nancy Reagan was fascinated by ideas and strategies. Ron and Nancy started a family almost immediately. Patricia Ann was born in 1952, and Ronald Prescott in 1958.

CAREER PROBLEMS

Marriage to Nancy brought Reagan enormous joy and emotional comfort, but it did not end his career troubles. In 1945, when he was discharged from the army and returned to his job in the motion picture

Reagan is pictured with his wife Nancy and their children Patti and Ron Jr. Reagan was a devoted husband and a loving—if sometimes distant—father.

industry, he confronted several staggering problems. To begin with, he was getting older, and had been largely AWOL from America's silver screens for three years. Newer actors, including Dana Andrews and Van Johnson, had risen to prominence. To younger moviegoers, *Kings Row* seemed like a relic of the silent era.

Hollywood, furthermore, was confronting devastating troubles of its own. The leaders of the major studios had built their empires on a monopolistic business model that allowed them to control the production, distribution, and exhibition of feature films. Their reach even extended to theater bookings and ticket pricing. And to a large measure, they had successfully stunted the growth of foreign competition, opening the world to their product. This cozy, profitable arrangement ended not long after the conclusion of the war. The Supreme Court's 1948 *Paramount* decision ended such lucrative practices as block booking and price-fixing. Soon after, the court ordered the studios to sell off their theaters, to separate their production and distribution divisions from their exhibition arm.

While the courts were ending business as usual for the moguls, Hollywood was losing a large part of its audience. The rise of the British, French, and Italian film industries cut into Hollywood's foreign market, and at the same time, technological and demographic changes began to reduce the American film audience. In 1947 television began its commercial expansion. That year, there were 14,000 television sets in the country; by 1954 there were 32 million. By the end of the 1950s, nearly 90 percent of homes in America had at least one television. Adding to Hollywood's woes, during those same years, millions of Americans moved to the suburbs, began families, and enjoyed a rich variety of entertainment options. During this time of dramatic change in the country, for Hollywood the bottom line was that movie attendance was cut in half.

Ronald Reagan was one of thousands of workers in the motion picture industry caught in the crunch. The studios eliminated or slashed their B-film divisions and made fewer feature films, which in turn were seen by fewer people as the moviegoing population declined even further. The motto of the moment was: be big or be out. Some of the biggest stars—including Humphrey Bogart, Jimmy Stewart, Burt Lancaster, Kirk Douglas, and John Wayne—ventured into independent production. Large numbers of industry employees—actors as well as directors, writers, and technicians—lost their jobs and were forced out of the business.

Back at Warner Bros., Reagan struggled to regain his status. Westerns were becoming increasingly popular, and, like Stewart and Wayne, he hoped to move in that direction for any potential roles. He rode a horse beautifully, and he had the ideal look for the genre: a ruggedly handsome face with a hard, narrow-eyed stare. Before the war Reagan was known for his inviting smile and pleasing profile, but upon his return, a few years of experience and maturity had given him a tougher—yet still handsome—look.

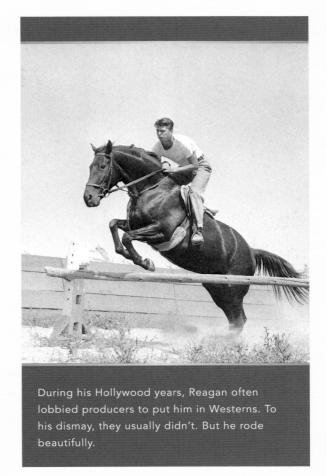

During his Hollywood years, Reagan often lobbied producers to put him in Westerns. To his dismay, they usually didn't. But he rode beautifully.

However, Warner Bros. had different ideas for Reagan's postwar career. In *Stallion Road* (1947), his first role after the war, he rode a horse but didn't handle a gun. He played a veterinarian who saved livestock from an anthrax outbreak. The result was pleasing enough, mixing medicine and light romance, but it was not the star-making vehicle that Reagan needed. At a time when Wayne and Henry Fonda were making *Fort Apache* and Wayne and Montgomery Clift were starring in *Red River*, *Stallion Road* was an oater of a lesser breed.

It got worse. Against Reagan's repeated protests, Warner Bros. cast him opposite Shirley Temple in a shameless soap opera entitled *That Hagen Girl* (1947). From 1935 to 1938, Temple

For an actor who wanted to star in Westerns and action films, being cast as Shirley Temple's co-star in *That Hagen Girl* (1947) was disappointing. The film was one of Reagan's least favorite.

was not simply the most popular child actor in America, she was the biggest box office draw in the world. As a young girl, she was the embodiment of "cute," but as an adult actress she never made the transition to "gorgeous." Her career faltered. For her, as well as for Reagan, starring in *That Hagen Girl* was a career mistake. Reagan resented having to play a man in love with a woman half his age, and Temple was frustrated with a script that was riddled with contradictions.

Reagan's instincts were vindicated at the sneak preview. As he later wrote, "Came the moment on screen when I said to Shirley, 'I love you,' and the entire audience en masse cried, 'Oh, no!'" Although the line was edited out of the film, Dutch could not edit the film out of his life. At a time when Warner Bros. was beginning to cut production costs and reevaluate all of their "properties," *Stallion Road* and *That Hagen Girl* gave no indications that Reagan's star was rising.

His complaints were similar to other actors struggling to build (or revive) their careers after the war: weak roles and inferior directors. For the most part, Reagan got the scraps from the studio's plate. *The Voice of the Turtle* (1947) was a light, stagy comedy; *John Loves Mary* (1949) is almost its mirror image. In the 1947 film, Reagan played a soldier on furlough; in the 1949 one, he was cast as a returning veteran. For audiences of the late 1940s, the theme of returning soldiers was stale. Neither film did anything to resurrect his career.

By 1950, the marriage between Reagan and Warner Bros. was on the rocks. When the studio passed him over for a juicy part in a Western, he reached the breaking point. He wired Jack Warner, "I've always been good and done everything you asked—even *That Hagen Girl*." That loyalty, he insisted, had not been returned.

Agent Lew Wasserman finalized the divorce. Warner Bros., like other studios, was moving away from the contract system, and they released Reagan from his existing deal. For half of his salary, he agreed to make one picture a year for the studio. Beyond that commitment, he was a free agent. Wasserman quickly arranged a five-picture deal for Dutch at Universal. The studio, known mostly for horror films and other low-budget productions, agreed to pay Reagan $75,000 per picture.

Nearing the age of forty, Reagan had few illusions about his position in the Hollywood hierarchy. Some male movie stars reach such a height that in their forties and fifties they still can play leading roles. For Wayne, Bogart, Stewart, Peck, and Grant, age lines and thinning hair did little to diminish their appeal. Dutch never achieved that level of stardom, nor had he transitioned into true character-actor roles. In the early 1950s, he was an aging leading man, and like many baseball players

NOTABLE FILMS

1947
Stallion Road
That Hagen Girl
The Voice of the Turtle

1949
John Loves Mary
Night unto Night
The Girl from Jones Beach
The Hasty Heart

1950
Louisa

1951
Storm Warning
Bedtime for Bonzo
The Last Outpost

1952
Hong Kong
She's Working Her Way Through College
The Winning Team

1953
Tropic Zone
Law and Order

1954
Prisoner of War
Cattle Queen of Montana

1955
Tennessee's Partner

1957
Hellcats of the Navy

1961
The Young Doctors

1964
The Killers

near the end of the line, he finished his career with dignity and professionalism.

At Universal, Reagan starred in a few delightful, light comedies, including *Louisa* (1950) and the unjustly maligned *Bedtime for Bonzo* (1951). He also finally got his shot at Westerns. Although

After Reagan split with Warner Bros., he received a few roles in Westerns. In *Law and Order* (1953), a conventional, well-made Western, Reagan co-starred with Dorothy Malone.

none of these Westerns compared to the best in the genre (those by John Ford or Howard Hawks), Reagan's work in *The Last Outpost* (1951), *Law and Order* (1953), *Cattle Queen of Montana* (1954), and *Tennessee's Partner* (1955) demonstrated his talent as a believable Western actor. Most fittingly, he played baseball great Grover Cleveland Alexander in *The Winning Team* (1952). *Knute Rockne, All American* (1940) introduced a young, innocent Dutch Reagan to American moviegoers. *The Winning Team*—about an aging ballplayer seeking redemption—seems to say good-bye to Ronald Reagan, his face lined with age, his body failing, but, in the end, his hope undiminished.

Reagan's political critics never tired of mentioning that he co-starred with a chimpanzee in *Bedtime for Bonzo* (1951).

In *The Winning Team* (1952), Reagan played Grover Cleveland Alexander, the successful but troubled pitcher. The film had both baseball action and pathos. It was Reagan's final film for Warner Bros.

POLITICAL PASSIONS

Well before the end of his film career, Reagan revived another passion—politics, which had always been an interest of his. He had been active in high school and college politics, and throughout most of his years in Hollywood he had been an outspoken New Deal Democrat. He believed President Franklin D. Roosevelt had returned dignity to the working man, pulled the country out of the Great Depression, and saved democracy. During the war he joined and became active in the left-wing Hollywood Democratic Committee. Later rechristened the Hollywood Independent Citizens Committee of the Arts, Sciences, and Professions

In the late 1940s, Ronald Reagan became increasingly involved in the politics of the motion picture industry. In 1947, he became president of the Screen Actors Guild. He went on to serve seven more one-year terms as SAG president.

(HICCASP), the organization moved further to the left as time passed. Reagan also joined the American Veterans Committee, another leftist political organization.

After the war, he continued to support and to speak out in favor of liberal/leftist political causes. Always interested in foreign affairs, he condemned the mistreatment of Japanese Americans, opposed U.S. support for Chiang Kai-shek in the Chinese civil war, and criticized colonialism around the world. Reagan's political passions and abilities did not go unnoticed. Liberal Democrats encouraged him to run for Congress, and the FBI commented in his file that he had a record of "Communist activity and sympathies."

The FBI was wrong. Reagan's activities and sympathies were liberal, but never communist. It was the nature of the left in Hollywood that liberals and communists joined the same organizations, fought for the same causes, and often spoke with a single political voice. This mixing of political goals and ideological agendas virtually ended with the coming of the Cold War. At HICCASP meetings, Reagan watched how the communist members worked tirelessly to control the organization—how they "come early and stayed late," used democratic rules to delay votes and achieve undemocratic ends, and outshouted and outbullied their liberal opponents. He soon became disenchanted with HICCASP and dropped out, but the experience influenced his political thinking. He had seen the enemy, and it wasn't the Republicans in Hollywood or America. It was the communists who infiltrated and undermined liberal organizations; it was the Soviet Union who gave the marching orders to the American Communist Party.

What Reagan witnessed during his time with HICCASP colored his work in SAG. He became a SAG member soon after he arrived in Hollywood, and in 1941 became a member of its board. He left the board during his service years but resumed his position in 1945 on his return. In 1947, after George Montgomery resigned as president of SAG, Reagan was elected to replace him. The membership of the guild would subsequently reelect Reagan to seven more one-year terms (1947–1952 and 1959). During these years, the most politically divisive in the industry's history—a time that witnessed the Red Scare and the Hollywood Blacklist, as well as violent labor battles and economic troubles—Ronald

As SAG president, Reagan discusses the organization's issues with Nancy Reagan and James Cagney.

Ronald Reagan testified before the House Un-American Activities Committee (HUAC) in 1947. Because of his anticommunist position, Congress considered Reagan to be a friendly witness.

"Ninety-nine percent of us are pretty well aware of what is going on, and I think within the bounds of our democratic rights, and never once stepping over the rights given us by democracy, we have done a pretty good job in our business of keeping those people's activities curtailed. After all, we must recognize them at present as a political party . . .

"As a citizen I would hesitate, or not like, to see any political party outlawed on the basis of its political ideology. We have spent 170 years in this country on the basis that democracy is strong enough to stand up and fight against the inroads of any ideology. However, if it is proven that an organization is an agent of a power, a foreign power, or in any way not a legitimate political party, and I think the government is capable of proving that, if the proof is there, then that is another matter . . . "

—*RWR, congressional testimony, October 1947*

Reagan became the most compelling voice among actors, with the most visible profile. His years as the president of SAG also began his transformation from a liberal Democrat to a conservative Republican.

Unlike the Screen Writers Guild (SWG), SAG never ventured too far to the political left. Prior to Reagan taking office, SAG's previous two presidents, George Murphy and Robert Montgomery, had been bedrock conservatives, more interested in advancing the economic positions of actors than in changing the world. During his years as SAG's head, Reagan grew to share many of Murphy's and Montgomery's political positions, especially their fervent anticommunism.

Two of the most important events during Reagan's SAG leadership demonstrate his anticommunist stance. The first was a complex labor dispute between two trade organizations, the International Alliance of Theatrical Stage Employees and Motion Picture Operators (IATSE) and the Conference of Studio Unions (CSU). IATSE was tainted by its associations with the mob, as was CSU by its ties to communism. Reagan sided with IATSE and risked personal danger when he crossed a CSU picket line to go to work at Warner Bros. His actions prompted serious enough threats from CSU thugs that Warner Bros. assigned him an armed bodyguard.

At the time, Reagan maintained that his actions did not call into question his liberal credentials. He supported Democrat Harry Truman in the 1948 presidential election. He maintained that his battle was against communists, not liberals. "Tyranny is tyranny, and whether it comes from the right, left, or center, it is evil," he said.

His second stand against communist inroads in the film industry occurred in 1947 when the House Un-American Activities Committee (HUAC) investigated Hollywood. He appeared before HUAC as a "friendly" witness, but did not name names and denied that communists had used motion pictures to spread propaganda. Publicly, he called for the rule of law and the protection of civil liberties, but in private meetings with the FBI, he did name names.

A CONSERVATIVE FORCE

In the years after the union battles and the HUAC hearings, Reagan completed his political odyssey from liberal to conservative. Chronic financial problems—brought on, he believed, by a progressive tax structure that taxed the wealthiest Americans at a 91 percent rate—nudged him in that direction. Exposure to conservative business leaders also influenced him. As his film career declined and his earning ability flagged, he in effect joined the enemy. Like other displaced refugees from Hollywood, he accepted jobs in television. From 1954 to 1962 he hosted CBS's *General Electric Theater*, a dramatic anthology series. In addition to introducing weekly shows and serving as a GE spokesman, he occasionally starred in episodes. The show was eclectic, ranging from biblical period dramas and heavy melodramas to light comedies and Westerns. The show attracted leading talents,

The day before giving his testimony before HUAC, Reagan huddles with actors George Murphy and Robert Montgomery and HUAC counsel Robert E. Stripling.

In 1958 Ronald Reagan and Nancy Davis appeared in a *General Electric Theater* production entitled "A Turkey for the President." It did not revive either of their acting careers.

Reagan took over for Andrews, hosting the program from 1964 to 1966, departing only after he was elected governor of Death Valley and the rest of California.

Reagan's association with GE was especially important in formulating his conservative beliefs. He later half-jokingly called it his "postgraduate education in political science." As a pitchman for GE, Reagan traveled across the country giving speeches, meeting and listening to employees and clients, and reading conservative literature. When he began hosting *General Electric Theater,* he said he was a "hard-core New Dealer." During the next eight years, that hard core melted. By the time the show went off the air in 1962, Reagan had fully embraced conservatism and the Republican Party.

By then Reagan had a new set of core beliefs. Bitterly anticommunist in foreign policy, he had become an equally strident believer in the idea that lower taxes stimulated economic growth and that corporations like General Electric and General Motors made a positive contribution to the health and welfare of America. On the road with General Electric, his job was to convince people across the country that unbridled capitalism was America's gift to the world. And convince them he did. With disarming charm, an easy smile, and abundant wit, Reagan traveled the country delivering a message so sweet that it never tasted like medicine. The speech he fashioned and delivered countless times during those travels would soon change America.

including Broderick Crawford, Tony Curtis, Barry Fitzgerald, Jane Wyman, Bette Davis, and Barbara Stanwyck. It also provided GE with a charismatic pitch man for the company's products.

When *General Electric Theater* left the air, Reagan accepted a similar hosting position on *Death Valley Days*, an anthology of "real-life" Western dramas. Sponsored by 20 Mule Team Borax, the half-hour program had begun as a radio show in 1930 and moved to television in 1952. From 1952 to 1964 it was hosted by Stanley Andrews, "the Old Ranger," who would comment on Death Valley during the days of the Old West.

Although he remained the host of *General Electric Theater*, by 1960 Reagan was considering a move into the larger political world. Once a New Deal Democrat, Reagan had by now made the transition to Republican conservative.

Ronald Reagan introduces the CELEBRITY: "This General Electric portable television packs console performance into a 19-inch set at a sweet, low price. Why, the Celebrity works wherever a console will with its mighty new chassis and full-power transformer. And what a picture! Daylight Blue. The same crisp beauty you see on the noblest General Electric consoles." And built to live up to General Electric's record of trustworthiness: a study of television sets over a three-year period proved that General Electric sets needed less service than any other leading brand. All this for only $159.95. More, too—for a limited time only, most General Electric dealers are offering a smart plaid carry-cover with the Celebrity portable. See this star perform . . . today. **$159.95**

NEW 19-INCH PORTABLE

Progress Is Our Most Important Product

GENERAL ELECTRIC

TELEVISION RECEIVER DEPT., SYRACUSE, NEW YORK

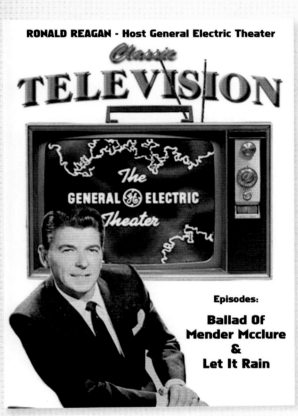

RONALD REAGAN - Host General Electric Theater

Classic

TELEVISION

The GENERAL GE ELECTRIC Theater

Episodes:

Ballad Of Mender Mcclure & Let It Rain

Newest guide for home buyers—the Live Better Electrically MEDALLION

This new Medallion assures you a home has been inspected by the local electric utility...meets modern standards for wiring, appliances and lighting. Look for the Medallion. It means a wonderful new way of life for you and your family!

What Sterling is to silver...that's what this Medallion is to a new house! It's the new national symbol of the finest in electrical living. Let these three top TV stars, speaking here for the electrical industry, tell how you save trouble, time, and money by choosing a home that wears the new Live Better Electrically Medallion.

BETTY: In a Medallion home, you start right off with a modern electric range, plus at least 3 additional major appliances, may be more. They're installed, ready to go to work the day you move in! Appliances are easier to pay for this way.

RONNIE: The lighting in every Medallion home is specially planned, too. It provides better light for better sight, plus new beauty for your home. You also get full Housepower. This means enough power, wiring, circuits, switches, and outlets to handle all the appliances you want to use.

FRAN: You'll be glad all your life you bought a Medallion home. Read below what a few of the thousands of new Medallion home owners think of them. Then go see the Medallion homes in your neighborhood. Your electric utility will tell you where they are.

New Ideas for Better Living

The new Medallion is backed up by home builders, electric utilities, and electrical manufacturers (Frigidaire, General Electric, Hotpoint, Kelvinator, Thermador, Westinghouse, Whirlpool, and others). This year, utilities will award Medallions to 100,000 new homes — in every style and price range across the country. You can see lots of new ideas for better living in the Medallion homes on display now!

YOU GET WONDERFUL FEATURES LIKE THESE IN MEDALLION HOMES!

ELECTRIC APPLIANCE. Mrs. Stanley Johnson, Arlington Heights, Ill.: "I just love our Medallion home — especially the kitchen. All those electric appliances that came with it — like this wall oven — sure make my job much easier. And my husband says they're easier to buy this way, because we pay for them on the mortgage."

LIGHT FOR LIVING. Mr. and Mrs. Charles B. McCarty, Greensboro, N. C.: "We never knew you could do so many beautiful things with lighting until we bought a Medallion home. Valance lighting, for example, makes our furniture and drapes look wonderful — and at the same time gives our son a well-lighted place to practice the piano."

FULL HOUSEPOWER. Mrs. Nick Pasquiello, Meriden, Conn.: "One of the things I like most in my Medallion home is all the handy outlets. I can plug in my portable cooking appliances wherever I want and use them — even with the washer going — without ever blowing a fuse. And I can cook a meal anywhere in the house — and outdoors, too."

ELECTRIC HEATING. Many Medallion homes feature electric heating, too. These are awarded a special Gold Medallion. The all-electric heat pump, shown here in the home of Mr. and Mrs. William Isaac of Beverly Hills, California, provides year-round comfort from a single unit which automatically heats or cools as the weather requires.

CHAPTER 5

GOVERNOR REAGAN

"I'VE NEVER PLAYED A GOVERNOR BEFORE."

—RWR

Ladies and gentlemen, we take pride in presenting a thoughtful address by Ronald Reagan," a peppy announcer declared on October 27, 1964, just one week before the presidential election. A studio audience watched the well-tanned actor—or was it former actor?—take his place behind a lectern. Simultaneously, a larger, more important audience was watching on NBC. The camera remained stationary while the crowd clapped respectfully. Reagan stood at frame left, too distant for television viewers to discern in any detail. A large poster of Arizona senator and Republican presidential candidate Barry Goldwater dominated the right side of the screen. The camera then swooped toward the dais, removing Goldwater from the frame. The next half hour belonged to Reagan alone.

Political moderates and liberals dismissed Reagan as a paranoid crank, if they paid him any attention at all. Now fully

No one gave political neophyte Ronald Reagan much of a chance in California's 1966 gubernatorial race. He proved them wrong, and not for the last time.

Barry Goldwater's (left) hard-line conservatism provided an early model for Reagan's own political philosophy.

was drawing enthusiastic crowds with essentially the same message. Unlike the senator, the actor had charisma. His soft smile smoothed his pointed rhetoric. He joked and cajoled, related humorous anecdotes fine-tuned to his audiences' desires, and delivered his lines with the easy charm of a man with twenty-five years of public speaking experience. Goldwater was a scold. Reagan was a winner.

A group of California businessmen aimed to bottle Reagan's magic. "We've got to get that speech on television," a wealthy auto dealer named Holmes Tuttle exclaimed after hearing Reagan at a fund-raiser in Los Angeles. He approached Reagan, who agreed to record a version of his stump speech in front of a studio audience.

A few weeks and a few million dollars delivered Reagan to a turning point in his life. Still dreaming of returning to acting and only just dipping a toe into politics, he had no inkling of this moment's significance. His prime-time talk, which later became known as "A Time for Choosing," rehashed ideas and language he had played with for a decade. He spoke not of Goldwater specifically (the candidate rated only an occasional mention), but rather of the general glories of conservatism. He blasted communism, which he saw as akin to satanism. He extolled capitalists as modern-day pioneers who spread freedom wherever they spent. And he denounced the federal government for standing in the way of progress. Reagan displayed a talent for reducing complex issues to cut-and-dried dualities where one side was obviously right and the other

identified as a Republican, he had made countless speeches on Goldwater's behalf over the past several months. Reagan wrote them himself using anecdotes and statistics culled from his long train rides around the country. Their virulent anticommunism and antigovernment rhetoric seemed overblown in those days of relative calm. Vietnam was hardly a blip on the American foreign policy radar. No one outside of Los Angeles had heard of Watts. Lyndon Johnson's Great Society remained a slogan rather than a program.

But change was in the air. Party insiders knew that Senator Goldwater's far-right campaign was doomed to electoral defeat in 1964. Reagan, however,

Not even Reagan's support could save Goldwater from a thumping in his 1964 presidential bid.

obviously wrong. "The issue of this election," he explained, was "whether we believe in the capacity for self-government or whether we abandon the American Revolution and confess that a little intellectual elite in a far-distant capital can plan our lives for us better than we can plan them ourselves."

That one sentence forged individualism, patriotism, anti-intellectualism, antiestablishmentism, and anticommunism into a unified message relevant to anyone who felt alienated, frightened, angry, betrayed, or stifled by America's postwar direction. The live audience ate it up, and so did viewers. Over eight million dollars in donations poured into the Republicans' coffers after the speech aired.

THE PULSE OF THE PEOPLE

Lyndon Johnson gave Goldwater one of the sternest drubbings in American electoral history. But during this time, Reagan had quickly emerged as a rising star within the conservative movement. Some true believers were already talking about a future run for the presidency. Perhaps he could achieve what Goldwater could not.

Holmes Tuttle and Reagan's other wealthy backers came calling within weeks of the election debacle. Run for governor, they begged. In what would become a pattern, Reagan asked for time to mull his options before committing. Elected office appealed to him, but he favored a run for the U.S. Senate or the House of Representatives. He knew little about state issues. Nancy doubted she would enjoy life as a politician's wife. The couple also worried about their finances, having become accustomed to a certain level of living. Tuttle assured Reagan that money would never be a problem. To prove it, Reagan's friends arranged a sweetheart deal whereby the Twentieth Century-Fox studio purchased his Santa Monica ranch for two million dollars (and later resold it at a massive loss).

Reagan sought advice from Spencer-Roberts, a high-powered political consulting team. They found the prospect of electing an actor intriguing. They also discovered that Reagan was an eager student who could take direction and stick to the script. Reagan's many well-received talks around California convinced him that he had an army waiting to march behind him. And he enjoyed all the fuss about him. He had all but decided to run for governor by mid-1965, when the first Friends of Ronald Reagan mailers started landing in mailboxes.

Centrist Republicans discouraged Reagan from running, fearing that he would split the party. He would also have to overcome Pat Brown, the two-term Democratic incumbent, an affable, moderate liberal who seemed a mortal lock for reelection. Under his leadership, California had become a model of mainstream liberalism. A racial progressive, Brown helped pass the Rumford Fair Housing Act, which barred Realtors and property owners from discriminating against nonwhite buyers and renters. He was a champion of the California Aqueduct, a vital if expensive system for the water-hungry state. Believing that education was essential for future growth, he oversaw a vast expansion of California's university system. An influx of new tax dollars built schools, expanded faculties, and guaranteed a free college education for every high school graduate in the state.

Where most saw progress, Reagan saw over-reach. "Keeping up with Governor Brown's promises is like trying to read *Playboy* magazine while your wife turns the pages," he joked.

Despite Brown's achievements, events over the past year had pushed California in Reagan's direction. Realtors denounced the Rumford Act as "forced housing." Property owners who sympathized with the civil rights struggle in Mississippi and other southern states objected when racial equality superseded what they saw as their inalienable property rights. Proposition 14, passed overwhelmingly in 1964 with Reagan's support, overturned the law.

Governor Brown's magnificent education system provided another source of social angst. Protests erupted at the University of California–Berkeley and at other campuses in response to Lyndon Johnson's expansion of the Vietnam War and school administrators' decisions to limit the free-speech rights of students. Brown sympathized with the demonstrators but believed he needed to quell the demonstrations. Police arrested hundreds of students. Sporadic, nonviolent uprisings

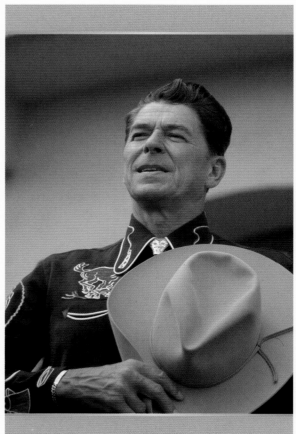

It takes a special kind of candidate to make this outrageous Western garb look natural.

continued, highlighted by a "filthy-speech movement" launched by a handful of Berkeley students in 1965. In most Californians' eyes, the movement's primary objective was to shout obscenities at as many people as possible.

California now found itself at the vanguard of deteriorating race relations. The emerging Black Power movement, which would not receive its name until 1966, was shifting the focus of racial unrest from abolishing segregation and increasing access to the ballot box toward questions of job discrimination and economic inequality. The Oakland-based Black Panthers, formed in 1966, would emerge as the most visible group within this element.

In August 1965, whites received a shock when race riots rocked the predominately black district of Los Angeles known as Watts. The disturbances began when police arrested a black man named Marquette Frye for driving while intoxicated. Frye's mother confronted the police and the situation escalated. Her protestations touched a nerve with area residents. Dozens, then hundreds, then thousands spilled into the streets complaining about the area's poor housing, lack of jobs, crumbling infrastructure, and history of police brutality. Governor Brown, who was vacationing in Greece, was unable to prevent the outbreak of violence. When the National Guard hesitated to assert control, rioters torched Watts. A week of looting and destruction resulted in thirty-four dead, a district in flames, and a dream of interracial harmony destroyed.

Reagan heard tales of discontent wherever he traveled. He found little sympathy for the students or the rioters. Instead, many voters were urging him to clean up "the mess at Berkeley." They fretted about intrusive government, the failure of law and order, and drug-addled kids taking to the streets. They saw a world out of control, and they yearned for someone to put things right again.

These were Reagan's people. With his instinct for reducing complex issues to black-and-white morality plays, he offered the kind of reassurance and tough talk that many Californians—Richard Nixon would eventually call them the "silent majority"—wanted.

THE LEADERSHIP GAP

Reagan declared his candidacy for governor on January 4, 1966. Governor Brown welcomed his entrance into the race. He felt that Reagan was too conservative to win the general election, and believed his campaign might well divide California Republicans.

Reagan cruised to an easy victory over San Francisco businessman George Christopher, his opponent in the primaries. On the advice of Spencer-Roberts, he framed himself as a "citizen-politician" whose inexperience shielded him from any connection to the corruption and cronyism that stalked Sacramento. Spencer-Roberts gave their client a crash course in the issues facing California; Reagan knew little about his home state, being far more interested in national politics. But he was a good crammer, even if he tended to ignore information that conflicted with what he already believed. His photographic memory enabled him to work from cue cards (actually four-by-six-inch index cards) while appearing to speak extemporaneously. His sharp wit and easygoing demeanor saved him whenever he flubbed tough questions from reporters.

Governor Brown, on the other hand, faced an unexpectedly tough primary challenge from Sam Yorty, the mayor of Los Angeles. Yorty attacked Brown from the right, accusing him of being too soft on lawbreakers and wayward students. Brown underestimated Yorty's appeal to law-and-order types, just as he underestimated Reagan. The governor won the Democratic primary, but in a less-than-convincing fashion.

Brown was a hobbled candidate as the general election campaign began. Reagan hammered away on social issues. Berkeley became his go-to applause line, his symbol for everything that Brown had mismanaged. He spoke of a "morality gap" between honest Americans and student protesters. "Who among us doesn't feel concern for the deterioration of old standards, the abandonment of principles time-tested and proved in our climb from the swamp to the stars?" he asked. He linked campus radicals with race rioters, arguing that both represented the breakdown of traditional morality, placing the ultimate blame on Governor Pat Brown. "There is a leadership gap, and a morality and decency gap in Sacramento," he argued, that had paved the way for "a small minority of beatniks, radicals, and filthy-speech advocates" to undermine tranquility.

Brown fought back as best he could. He never did reunite his party after the hard-fought primary, however. Nor did he truly grasp Reagan's widespread appeal until it was too late. His efforts to tar Reagan as an extremist smacked of desperation.

Reagan received over a million more votes than Brown. His calls for smaller government, a return to old-time values, and a renewed focus on law and order fused economic conservatives, social conservatives, and blue-collar Californians into a potent electoral force that would stand by him for the rest of his political career and beyond.

THE GOVERNOR

Ronald Reagan took the oath of office at 12:02 a.m. on January 2, 1967. Why the unusual time? He claimed that he wanted to prevent the outgoing governor from making last-minute judicial appointments. Skeptics noted that Brown had already spent two months doing just that, so an extra few hours were unlikely to make much difference. Perhaps Mrs. Reagan's astrologer thought it was a propitious time, they suggested.

Whatever the cause, Reagan's administration really began three days later, when he assembled his senior staff for the first time. "What do we do now?" he asked. This was a legitimate question. He had no idea how to be a governor. He had only the barest understanding of how to pass laws or deal with legislators. He had no specific

Reagan's message of law and order, patriotism, and small government played well in a state rocked by campus protests and race riots.

CALIFORNIA REPUBLIC

Reagan campaigns with the Red Garters Dixieland band in San Francisco, one of the centers of the counterculture movement that he denounced so strongly.

"Government is the people's business, and every man, woman and child becomes a shareholder with the first penny of tax paid. With all the profound wording of the Constitution, probably the most meaningful words are the first three, 'We, the People.'

"It is inconceivable to me that anyone could accept this delegated authority without asking God's help. I pray that we who legislate and administer will be granted wisdom and strength beyond our own limited power; that with divine guidance we can avoid easy expedients as we work to build a state where liberty under law and justice can triumph, where compassion can govern and wherein the people can participate and prosper because of their government and not in spite of it."

—*RWR, inaugural address, January 1967*

programs in mind, only a general sense of overall goals. Reagan was now the chief executive in charge of 115,000 public employees and responsible for 20 million Californians. Had it been its own country, California would have had the sixth-largest economy in the world.

Like an actor walking onto his first movie set, Governor Reagan put himself in the experts' hands. He trusted his advisors and department heads to handle day-to-day activities. California's professional bureaucracy would keep the schools open and the water flowing. As he saw it, his job was to lay out an overall agenda, not to immerse himself in nettlesome details. He was at heart a delegator who kept clear of political disputes unless absolutely necessary. Reagan was a manager, and a good one. The plaque over his office door epitomized how he interpreted his job: "OBSERVE THE RULES OR GET OUT."

Although Reagan adjusted to the governor's office with relative ease, he and Nancy struggled with the job's other obligations. The couple found Sacramento too sleepy for their tastes. It lacked the glitz, glamour, and good weather of Santa Monica, Beverly Hills, or Malibu. They spent most weekends at their home in Pacific Palisades.

Nancy hated the governor's mansion, a dilapidated pile that should have been condemned years earlier. It was on a busy street. Dry rot had gutted its framing. A rope in the Reagans' bedroom served as a fire escape. "That house was so depressing that I just couldn't stand the thought of living

California State Supreme Court justice Marshall F. McComb administers the oath of office to Governor Reagan on January 2, 1967, while the Reverend Wilbur Choy looks on.

there," she lamented. They lasted three months before renting a two-story Tudor in a posh section of east Sacramento.

Rough treatment from the press left Nancy regretting her husband's entrance into politics. Ronnie's gregarious charm insulated him from most negative coverage. You could disagree with him, but it was hard to dislike him. His sensitive wife, on the other hand, could not conjure up her husband's magic. Reporters typically depicted her as a brittle harpy. She sought solace in long baths, during which she staged imaginary and inevitably triumphant conversations with offending reporters.

Creaky floorboards and a cranky wife could not prevent Reagan from doing his job. He navigated several thorny issues during his two terms in Sacramento. To the surprise of many—and to the dismay of some—he revealed himself as more of a pragmatic politician than a strict ideologue.

Nowhere was this truer than in the area of taxes and spending. Reagan had entered office with a seemingly simple plan. "We are going to squeeze and cut and trim until we reduce the cost of government," he proclaimed during his predawn inaugural address. "It won't be easy and it won't be pleasant."

Reagan liked to joke that he had never played a governor before, but he quickly learned that competent department heads could handle the day-to-day operations of California's large public bureaucracy.

California was in serious fiscal trouble. Governor Brown had recognized that the state was facing budget deficits, but refrained from raising taxes during an election year. Reagan naively assumed that he could balance the budget by eliminating government waste, the exact nature of which he had never specifically identified. When that assumption proved false, he proposed slashing every department's budget by 10 percent regardless of the consequences. He quickly abandoned that idea, although some agencies did suffer tremendous cuts in his first budget, most notoriously the gutting of California's Department of Mental Hygiene, which eliminated thousands of jobs and weakened an already rickety mental-health system.

Reagan eventually embraced a more balanced approach to deficit reduction. As passed, his 1967 budget trimmed the spending of some agencies while imposing the largest tax increases in the state's history. In a demonstration of his keen political instincts, he escaped voter backlash by blaming the tax hikes on his predecessor's fiscal irresponsibility.

The governor proved equally pragmatic on education issues. The unrest at Berkeley had punched his ticket to Sacramento. He continued to use student protesters as foils whenever possible. His response to one bearded demonstrator at UC Santa

Cruz made headlines and drew applause. "We are the future!" the student screamed at the governor's limousine. From inside, Reagan jotted a message that he pressed against the window for the demonstrators to see: "I'll sell my bonds."

Reagan respected university professors and other highly educated people; he just wanted colleges to focus on learning rather than social revolution. The idea that combating social ills might be part of one's education never occurred to him, and he repeatedly took a hard line against demonstrators. In 1969, for example, he dispatched the California Highway Patrol and the National Guard to quell the "criminal anarchists" and "off-campus revolutionaries" he believed were disrupting the Berkeley campus. "If it takes a bloodbath, let's get it over with," he said the following year in response to renewed unrest. At the same time, spending on higher education more than doubled during Reagan's eight years in office. The governor also oversaw a vast increase in scholarship funding.

Governor Reagan also left a lasting, positive impact on California's wild places. Despite considering himself an outdoorsman, Reagan knew little about environmental issues. The modern environmentalist movement was in its infancy, with the first Earth Day celebration occurring in 1970. During a campaign speech to a group of

Student protesters and other liberals never embraced Reagan as governor. But his ability to disarm them with a quip and a smile proved important to his success.

lumber-company executives he had joked that "a tree is a tree—how many more do you need to look at?"

Most of the credit for Reagan's environmental achievements belongs to his Executive Director for Resources, Ike Livermore, a horse-riding business-man who saw himself as an ideological heir of the great conservationist Theodore Roosevelt. With Livermore leading him along, Reagan protected old-growth redwood forests, blocked projects to dam unfettered waterways, and signed tough air- and water-quality bills into law. California's park system grew by 145,000 acres during his administration.

Of all the questions Reagan faced during his first term, none tortured him more than the 1967 Therapeutic Abortion Bill. The Supreme Court's decision in *Roe v. Wade* was still six years away. Abortion lurked in the unregulated shadows. The 1967 measure permitted women to end their preg-nancies in cases of rape, incest, or endangerment to their health. "I just can't give you a decision," he stammered when reporters asked whether he would sign the bill. He consulted clergymen, who urged him to veto it, and his physician father-in-law, who urged him not to. After much wavering, and with much regret, he signed the Therapeutic Abortion

Nancy took media criticism personally. Her husband rolled with the punches. Although prone to gaffes, Reagan used his press conferences to advance his agenda by appealing directly to the people.

By 1974, Reagan was appearing at more political events outside of California than ever before. Insiders began to ask whether the genial governor was planning a run at the White House.

Bill into law. The number of legal abortions in California increased from 518 in 1967 to 199,089 in 1980.

Reagan was an effective executive who exchanged ideological purity for pragmatic leadership. He preferred to leave his office early so he could read or watch *Mission: Impossible* rather than stay late to pal around with legislators. He nevertheless worked well with members of both parties. His efforts on welfare reform exemplified his compromising spirit.

The number of welfare recipients in the state swelled from 375,000 in 1963 to 1,150,687 in 1969. Reagan decried the current system as a "welfare

monster." He believed that cheating and corruption permeated the system, and would say much the same during his presidency despite overwhelming evidence to the contrary.

A few months into his second term, he began discussions with Bob Moretti, the Democratic speaker of the state assembly. "Governor, I don't like you," Moretti said, "and I know you don't like me, but we don't have to be in love to work together." The two men spent weeks going back and forth in negotiations that reminded Reagan of his face-offs against studio executives during his days with SAG. Together they forged a landmark bill, the California Welfare Reform Act, which increased aid payments

Reagan stepped down in 1974 after two largely successful terms as governor. Despite his tough rhetoric, he had proven to be a pragmatic politician who often steered toward the middle when presented with contentious issues. Supporters wondered whether the same approach might work in Washington, D.C.

but tightened eligibility requirements. Reagan, not the Democrats, seized the credit when the welfare rolls began shrinking. That was part of Reagan's genius: the ability to declare victory even when he had gained only half a loaf.

Reagan left California a very different place than he had found it. The state's budget had more than doubled, leaping from $4.6 billion per year to $10.2 billion. Its tax system became more progressive due to higher income and corporate levies. Education spending increased, as did environmental protections. Unfortunately, so had crime rates. The murder rate doubled during Reagan's tenure despite a slew of tough anticrime laws.

Steady, competent leadership had transformed the one-time fringe candidate into a serious politician whose rhetorical gifts made him a darling of conservatives. His supporters convinced him to make a well-publicized, undeclared run for president in 1968 that he abandoned only when it became clear that fellow Californian Richard Nixon would win the nomination.

"As we left Sacramento," Nancy later wrote, "I honestly believed we were leaving politics forever." Her husband agreed, at least publicly. Yet Reagan spent much of 1974, his final full year in office, appearing on national television programs and delivering speeches around the country. His blasé demeanor had always concealed his driving ambition. With his sixty-fourth birthday approaching, Ronald Reagan didn't seem like a man pining for retirement.

1964–1975
TIMELINE

1964 Ronald Reagan's political career is effectively launched after his speech "A Time for Choosing" airs on prime-time television in support of Republican presidential candidate Senator Barry Goldwater.

1965 Reagan publishes his memoir, *Where's the Rest of Me?*

1966 Reagan is elected governor of California in a landslide victory over incumbent Pat Brown.

1967 The Reagans move out of the dilapidated governor's mansion and into a posh Tudor home in Sacramento.

1968 Reagan announces his candidacy for president at the Republican National Convention in Miami. After a brief campaign, Reagan drops out of the race when it becomes clear that Richard Nixon will win the nomination.

1969 The National Guard occupies the University of California at Berkeley campus for seventeen days, dispatched by Reagan to quell student demonstrations.

1970 Reagan is reelected governor of California over Democrat Jesse Unruh, the leader of the California Assembly.

1972 Richard Nixon wins reelection to the White House.

1973 In the midst of the Watergate scandal, Reagan shows support for Nixon.

1974 Nixon resigns under threat of impeachment and Vice President Gerald Ford assumes the presidency.

1975 Reagan finishes his term as governor of California and is succeeded by Democrat Jerry Brown.

CHAPTER 6

THE CANDIDATE

"NANCY VOTED FOR SOME HAS-BEEN ACTOR."

—RWR

A little old lady—no one ever did get her name—recognized Reagan on a January 1975 flight from San Francisco to Los Angeles. "You *gotta* run for president!" she demanded. Reagan clamped a smile on his face, as he always did when presented with an insistent stranger. He sank into thought as she returned to her seat. A few minutes later, he turned to his trusted aide Mike Deaver. "Mike," he said, "I guess I really do have to run." Deaver's eyes widened. "I've always been a player on the bench," Reagan explained. "It's time for me to get into the game."

The story might be true. Even if it isn't, it captures the mood surrounding the Reagan camp as he handed over California's governorship to Jerry Brown. Reagan mused about retiring to Rancho del Cielo, his new 688-acre property overlooking Santa Barbara, but his actions suggested something else. Once out of office, he disseminated his conservative message through a

Although his 1976 bid for the presidency came up short, Reagan stole the show at that year's Republican National Convention in Kansas City.

Daughter Maureen looks thrilled that Dad just announced his candidacy for the presidency. Always aware of the visuals, Reagan chose a suitable backdrop for the scene.

popular newspaper column (generally written by his staffers) and a three-minute daily radio broadcast that he wrote longhand on yellow legal pads. Over ten million people heard him each day. He also hit the lecture circuit, earning generous speaking fees for extolling the merits of the free enterprise system and lamenting the supposed decline of the old-fashioned work ethic. "Looking back," Nancy wrote in her memoirs, "I realize it was inevitable that Ronnie would run."

In normal times, a sixty-four-year-old former governor would never consider running against an incumbent president from his own party. But these were not normal times. Stagflation, a vicious combination of economic recession, high

unemployment rates, and rampant inflation, left Americans fearful about their future. The fall of Saigon in April 1975 marked a painful coda to the Vietnam War. Watergate's lingering stench further eroded Americans' faith in their political leadership.

President Gerald Ford, a good man thrown into an awful situation after Richard Nixon's resignation, proved unequal to the challenges he faced. Ford's pardon of the disgraced ex-president created public outrage. His "Whip Inflation Now" campaign, which consisted largely of wearing "W.I.N." buttons, could not tame the economy. Conservatives like Reagan recoiled when Ford appointed Nelson Rockefeller, a liberal Republican, as his vice president and presumptive heir. Religious conservatives howled when First Lady Betty Ford declared herself pro-choice on abortion.

THE INSURGENT

Reagan concluded that Ford just wasn't up to the job. He had Nancy summon the family on October 31, 1975. Maureen and Mike dutifully appeared. Patti, estranged from her father, didn't. Seventeen-year-old Ron fidgeted. While Nancy prepared her husband's Halloween costume, Reagan told the kids that he was running for president.

The public announcement came soon after. Gerald Ford couldn't believe it, having already considered, and dismissed, the prospect of a Reagan challenge for the presidency.

Reagan, an experienced campaigner at the state level, simply wasn't prepared for the scrutiny national candidates faced. His tendency to skim briefing materials and make up answers on the fly diminished his credibility. Reporters poked holes in his *Reader's Digest*–level understanding of issues. More damaging was a speech he had made back in September entitled "Let the People Rule" that proposed spinning off federal welfare, education, health, housing, and other programs to the states. America's problems "all stem from a single source: the belief that government, particularly the

Supporters in Los Angeles give Reagan a rapturous reception. Although he was the underdog, the candidate found appreciative crowds wherever he went.

Reagan knew he faced an uphill climb, but kept promoting his conservative vision as he campaigned around the country.

federal government, has the answer to our ills," he declared. After shedding these responsibilities, Reagan believed Washington could balance the budget, pay down the national debt, and slash income taxes.

Reagan offered a blueprint for dismantling the Great Society and the New Deal without thinking through the consequences. The problem was partly political. Candidates who describe specific programs in detail expose themselves to attacks. There were also fiscal difficulties in his proposals, as Reagan's so-called Ninety Billion plan would require states to levy massive tax hikes to cover

their new responsibilities. Reagan, who should have been prepared to address this concern, fumbled his way through a round of interviews. Largely because of this, President Ford won the New Hampshire primary, a contest Reagan had expected to win, by a mere 1,317 votes.

More bad news followed. Reagan lost in Florida and Illinois. Then Barry Goldwater, the conservative movement's hero, endorsed Ford. By this point, Reagan's campaign was almost broke. They downsized from a chartered jet to a yellow prop plane they nicknamed the Flying Banana. Mike Deaver distributed Kentucky Fried Chicken when the Banana landed. Yet Reagan still believed his candidacy could survive these setbacks. People who attended his rallies never questioned his "facts" because they believed in him as a person.

Reagan came alive once his back hit the wall. He promised to carry on to the convention despite the early primary losses. Every candidate says that, but he truly believed it. "I'm *not* going to quit," he growled. On the advice of his aides, he started pummeling Ford on foreign policy. Exuding his trademark optimism, he tapped into Americans' fears that they had entered an age of declining power. He falsely—but effectively—asserted that the Soviet Union had established military superiority over the United States. He criticized Ford and Secretary of State Henry Kissinger for continuing Richard Nixon's policy of détente, or improving relations, with the Soviets. Ford's pursuit of a treaty that would hand over the Panama Canal to Panama inspired Reagan's most effective applause line. "We bought it, we paid for it, it's ours, and we're going to keep it," he thundered in town after town.

These attacks, along with some magnificent television appearances, lifted Reagan's poll numbers. A surprise victory in North Carolina buoyed the campaign, setting the stage for more victories. Texas, Alabama, and Georgia swung behind him, as did the West, including California's rich haul of delegates.

By August 1976, when Republicans descended on Kansas City for their national convention, Reagan trailed Ford by just 63 delegates, 1,030 to 1,093, with 136 still uncommitted. In a surprise move, Reagan announced that Pennsylvania senator Richard Schweiker would be his running mate. Schweiker was more liberal than Reagan, who barely knew him. It was a pragmatic move aimed at attracting unattached delegates while forcing Ford into a corner.

Ford's handlers managed the convention well, ceding ground to conservatives when drafting the party's platform in exchange for votes and public harmony. With his chances slipping away, Reagan refused to fracture the convention for his own personal gain. "Honey," Nancy said after Ronnie came

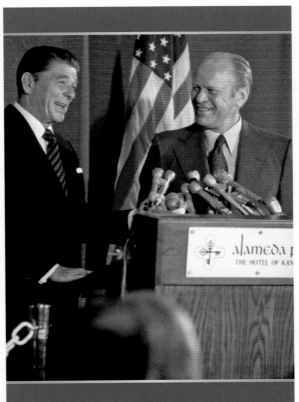

Although Reagan had concerns about President Ford's abilities, he doggedly campaigned for him throughout the 1976 general election season.

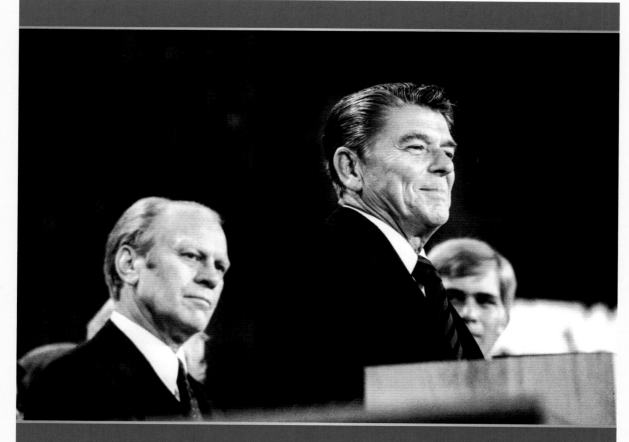

Reagan famously stole the spotlight from Gerald Ford at the 1976 Republican convention. As he spoke, the crowd was moved as Reagan recalled his thoughts when composing a note for a time capsule to be opened in 2076 at the country's tricentennial.

up short in the delegate count, "in all the years we've been married, you have never done anything to disappoint me. And I've never been prouder of you than I am now." Reagan handled the defeat with relative equanimity, smiling from his skybox and brushing off suggestions that he demand the vice-presidential slot. His poise and grace—his essential Reagan-ness—made him a president-in-waiting rather than simply a lovable loser.

THE HEIR APPARENT

Ford, after accepting the nomination, waved Reagan down to the stage. Historians have debated whether Reagan knew in advance that he would be asked to speak. What cannot be doubted is that he approached the stage with a memorized speech ready to go, just like all those lines he recited in sixty-nine movies and countless television appearances.

The crowd in Kemper Arena leapt to its feet, letting loose a roar that dwarfed the ovation for the actual nominee, Gerald Ford. Then an awestruck silence enveloped the room as the tanned, smiling Reagan, looking crisp in a dark suit and red-and-blue striped tie, prepared to speak. He threw some obligatory plaudits at Ford, without saying the president's name, before applauding the convention's lurch to the political right. "I believe the Republican Party has a platform that is a banner of bold, unmistakable colors, with no pale pastel shades," he declared to great cheers. He was echoing the mantra that brought him such success in 1966, when as a gubernatorial candidate he divided California into real Americans and disloyal troublemakers rather than explore the gray area in between.

Thousands stood in rapture. Some clasped their hands and others wiped tears from their eyes when Reagan abruptly shifted rhetorical gears—as if ad-libbing, but surely planned. He told the crowd that he had been recently asked to contribute a note for a time capsule to be opened at America's tricentennial, in 2076. At first, he considered writing about "the challenges confronting us, the erosion of freedom that has taken place under Democrat rule, the invasion of private rights, the controls and restrictions on the vitality of the great free economy that we enjoy."

But no, he continued. There was a more pressing issue. Nuclear Armageddon hangs over us all. Future Americans, he told the audience, would already know whether we had made the right choices. "Will they look back with appreciation and say, 'Thank God for those people in 1976 who headed off that loss of freedom, who kept us now a hundred years later free, who kept our world from nuclear destruction?" he asked. "This is our challenge," he concluded. "We must go forth from here united, determined that what a great general said a few years ago is true: there is no substitute for victory, Mr. President."

Ron and Nancy stop to thank admirers on their way to the podium at the 1976 Republican National Convention at Kemper Arena in Kansas City.

Gerald Ford could only dream of getting the kind of adoration Reagan received. Network cameras fixed on the Californian as he shook delegates' hands with that peculiar, "aw-shucks" expression on his face. The stage, filled with the extended families of both Ford and his vice-presidential candidate, Bob Dole, felt curiously empty once Reagan departed.

Ron and Nancy left Kansas City the next morning. On their way to the airport they passed a sign reading "Good-bye, Republicans. You picked the wrong man." Reagan played the good soldier by campaigning for Ford throughout the fall of 1976.

The president nevertheless lost to former Georgia governor Jimmy Carter, whose infectious grin and outside-the-beltway demeanor made him a perfect tonic for a nation wearied by Vietnam, Watergate, and stagflation. It was a close election; Carter won with a 297–240 electoral vote count. The South, which had been trending Republican, provided the native son's margin of victory.

ANOTHER RUN

But even before Carter took the oath of office, Reagan was already planning for 1980. He worked the lecture circuit, resumed his newspaper columns and radio broadcasts, and invited strategists to Rancho del Cielo.

Although he dared not declare his candidacy too soon lest he expose himself to attacks, Reagan knew the country was bending in his favor. The inflation rate reached 9.1 percent in 1978, with no signs of abating. Unemployment remained high. Oil prices spiked when the Shah of Iran, an anti-communist autocrat installed during a CIA coup in 1953, fled amid rising protests. His successor, the Ayatollah Khomeini, a stern, Islamic fundamentalist bent on establishing a theocracy, smiled when a mob of Iranian students took fifty-two Americans hostage in November 1979. Americans sank into an even deeper funk when the Soviet Union invaded Afghanistan the following month.

Antigovernment sentiments roiled the country. Blue-collar workers, angered by the transfer of manufacturing jobs overseas, concluded that Washington cared more about coddling criminals and appeasing social revolutionaries than it did about them. Well-financed right-wing think tanks such as the American Enterprise Institute and the Heritage Foundation churned out torrents of conservative literature and model legislation. Evangelical conservatives, seeing freer attitudes toward sex and drugs as evidence of a dangerously secularized society, mobilized behind such evangelical Republican allies as Reverend Jerry Falwell and his Moral Majority, which lobbied for laws that promoted the social priorities of conservative Christians. And in California, voters overwhelmingly approved Proposition 13, which slashed property tax rates while requiring a two-thirds legislative majority to raise taxes in the future.

President Jimmy Carter's approval rating hovered around 32 percent when Reagan officially announced his candidacy on November 13, 1979. He was the clear front-runner in a crowded Republican field. The campaign's first few months had the air of a coronation as he jetted around the country more intent on proving his vigor than his readiness. As in 1976, his lack of preparation produced many gaffes and half-baked answers. "Ronnie's friendly and casual style occasionally got him in trouble," Nancy allowed.

Reagan's team blundered in the crucial early state of Iowa. The candidate made several quick visits but never engaged in the kind of door-to-door, retail politics that Iowa caucus voters expected. Former congressman, United Nations

Reagan was ready to declare his candidacy by late 1979. With a sagging economy and an electorate weary of overseas troubles, incumbent Jimmy Carter seemed vulnerable.

ambassador, and CIA director George H. W. Bush, who was emerging as Reagan's sternest competition, bragged that he had spent more days in Iowa than Reagan had hours. Bush squeaked out a 2,182-vote victory.

As in 1976, Reagan rededicated himself to his campaign after an early stinging defeat in Iowa. Newly energized, he dominated a seven-man debate in New Hampshire not with superior knowledge but with his trademark remarkable charm. The field may have been crowded, but he was the only candidate with charisma.

With his poll numbers soaring, Reagan sparred with the Bush campaign over the rules for a second New Hampshire debate. The Bush camp preferred a one-on-one matchup. Reagan offered to pay for the event himself if the other Republican candidates could participate (thereby making it more difficult for Bush to focus on him). On the night of the debate, Bush stared blankly forward while Reagan arranged the other, nonviable candidates behind him on the stage. *Nashua Telegraph* editor and debate moderator Jon Breen struggled to restore order in the tumultuous gymnasium.

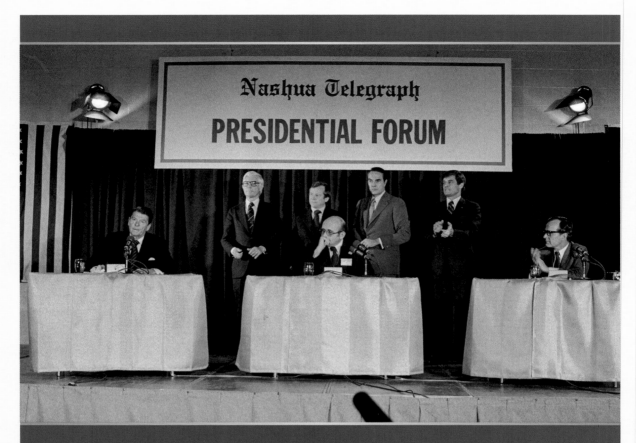

Republican presidential candidate George H. W. Bush (right) looks like he would rather be anywhere than Nashua, New Hampshire, after Reagan produced the candidates that had previously been excluded from their debate. Behind moderator Jon Breen are (left to right) candidates John Anderson, Howard Baker, Bob Dole, and Philip Crane.

Reagan had just started explaining his actions when Breen requested that his microphone be shut off.

"I am paying for this microphone, Mr. Green," Reagan retorted, his face flushed with anger. The crowd went wild, their cheers burying Reagan's flubbing of his antagonist's name. "You tell him, honey, you tell him!" Nancy shouted from her seat. From the fourth row, *Washington Post* correspondent David Broder muttered, "Reagan is winning this primary right now."

Broder was right. Reagan crushed Bush and all the other candidates in New Hampshire. The Gipper was back. Fringe candidates melted away until it became a two-horse race between Reagan and Bush. Reagan's victory in the Illinois primary in March 1980 made the nomination all but inevitable.

A celebratory mood gripped the campaign. Nancy developed a ritual of rolling an orange down the aisle when their plane (now a proper jet instead of the Yellow Banana) took off. Reporters good-naturedly constructed obstacle courses to keep the orange from reaching the back of the plane. In that same fun-loving spirit, the pilot kept a rubber chicken in the cockpit. He stuck it in the window whenever they landed, then tried to convince air-traffic controllers that the plane had hit a bird during its descent.

Reagan held Bush in low regard. He found the Yale graduate too stiff, too formal, and too prone to wilting under pressure, as he had in Nashua. The pair certainly made an interesting contrast. Bush looked every inch like an old-style, establishment Republican. His bloodlines were pure, his education impeccable, and his suits immaculate. Reagan, for all his years, resembled something new. He was a cowboy hero from the emerging Sunbelt who had pulled himself up by his bootstraps and spoke in terms any farmer or steelworker could understand.

Reagan may have doubted Bush's fortitude, but he valued party unity. At the Republican convention, after flirting with the idea of a Reagan-Ford "dream team," he asked Bush to be his running mate.

George H. W. Bush questioned Reagan's economic positions but accepted his offer to become his running mate.

The moment that every politician dreams of. Ronald Reagan accepts the Republican Party's nomination at its national convention in Detroit in 1980.

ARE YOU HAPPIER TODAY?

Jimmy Carter had lamented a national "crisis of confidence" in a July 1979 speech. Unfortunately for the president, as the election neared, he proved unable to lift the nation's bleak mood. The hostages were still in Iran, and the Russians remained in Afghanistan. Interest rates were sky-high as part of Federal Reserve Chairman Paul Volcker's effort to suffocate inflation. Volcker's policies ultimately bore fruit, but not until after it was too late for Carter to reap any of the benefits. Carter spoke in grim terms about a new era of limitations in which Americans needed to rein in their expectations. They needed to put on a sweater and turn down their thermostats, and to accept higher gas prices and the new 55 mph speed limit. Earnest though he was, the president came off like a lecturer-in-chief. The nation wanted inspiration, not scolding.

Reagan's innate optimism sharpened the contrast with his opponent. Even so, a series of missteps nearly blew his lead in the polls. His full-throated defense of states' rights before a mostly white crowd in Philadelphia, Mississippi, the site of the brutal murder of three civil rights workers in 1964, raised uncomfortable reminders of segregation. And a fence-mending visit to the South Bronx drew jeers from minority onlookers. Reagan's verbal miscues continued, most notoriously—and bewilderingly—when he asserted that "sixteen permanent oil slicks" floating off the coast of Santa Barbara had been scrubbing pollution from the air for "as long as the memory of man." One aide commented that "the only good news for us at this time is that we were making so many blunders that reporters had to pick and choose which ones they would write about."

The candidates were running neck and neck by Labor Day. Carter's latest accusations—that Reagan was a racist and a warmonger—had gained some traction. But Reagan's gibe that "a recession is when your neighbor loses his job, a depression is when you lose yours, and recovery is when Jimmy Carter loses his," gained more. Polling in Texas, California, and other key states suggested a Republican win. Still, Reagan worried that an October surprise, such as a deal to free the hostages from Iran, might reverse the tide.

The lone presidential debate, staged on October 28, less than a week before the election, offered a perfect opportunity for Reagan to seal the deal. He

Not for the last time in his political career, Reagan has a strategically placed symbol of American liberty looking over his shoulder.

Reagan and Bush make a pledge to the nation on this 1980 campaign button.

Showing off a gift from an admirer at the Michigan State Fair. Reagan successfully cast himself as an embodiment of homespun values and frontier traditions.

Candidate Reagan drops in on a neighborhood barbecue in Michigan. His ability to connect with blue-collar voters proved essential to his eventual victory.

was nervous, as he often was before debates, but capably sold himself as a peace-loving grandfather. He dismissed Carter's assertion that supply-side economics, a program of deep tax cuts and reduced government spending that Reagan had recently embraced, would open enormous budget deficits and hurt the poor.

More than anything, Reagan benefited from the contrast between the two men. Carter doggedly cited facts and statistics, hoping to make his case through sheer force of preparation. Reagan appeared loose and joyful, engaging viewers with one-liners and stories rather than nuanced policy arguments, which he figured would soon be forgotten anyway.

The debate's most memorable moment, and perhaps its only memorable moment, came when Carter criticized Reagan for opposing Medicare back in the 1960s. Reagan was laughing before Carter even finished. He had focused his debate prep on polishing zingers, not memorizing briefing books, and he had one ready to go.

Reagan hammers the final nail into President Jimmy Carter's political coffin at the presidential debate on October 28, 1980, less than a week before Election Day.

After his winning performance in the debate with President Carter, Reagan gives a big thumbs-up to his supporters with Nancy by his side.

"There you go again," he smiled. Had images of *Dark Victory*, with his exasperated "here we go again," flashed through his mind?

Polls showed that Reagan won the debate by an overwhelming margin. A double rainbow arced over his birthplace of Tampico, Illinois, on the eve of the election, as if to confer a celestial blessing on his candidacy.

"Are you happier today than when Mr. Carter became president of the United States?" Reagan asked during the debate. The American people decided they were not. Reagan amassed 489 electoral votes, compared to Carter's 80. Reagan won just 50.8 percent of the popular vote, hardly a mandate (6.6 percent of voters checked liberal Republican John Anderson's box). This was an anti-Carter vote, not a pro-Reagan one. In fact, exit polls showed that only 11 percent of voters supported Reagan because he was a conservative.

Clearly, Reagan still had a lot of convincing to do to win over the American people and to secure his legacy. But now it was time to celebrate. Ronald Reagan, through a combination of relentless ambition, inherent talent, and sheer luck, had completed an unlikely journey from small-town dreamer to president of the United States.

"I bet there's a hot time in Dixon tonight," his brother Neil joked.

"I'd like to be there off in a corner just listening," the president-elect replied.

Columbia, South Carolina, gives Ron and Nancy a warm greeting. With his extensive background in entertainment, Reagan had an instinctive gift for finding photo-friendly moments like this one.

Dixon becomes the new Plains, Georgia

Dixon Evening Telegraph

Wednesday, Nov. 5, 1980

Weather outlook: Sunny

Reagan wins by landslide

Dixonites go wild with joy

President elect Ronald Reagan is all smiles at the Century Plaza Hotel where he gave his victory speech. (UPI Photo)

By the rockets red glare and the bombs bursting in air, Dixon celebrated the election Tuesday night of one of its own as president — Ronald Reagan.

By the thousands they roared, shoved and swayed to a cacophony of rock music on First Street. They muscled in on a bandstand at the intersection of Hennepin Avenue and First Street and packed the downtown saloons.

A little more than an hour after President Carter conceded defeat, fireworks sparkled in the sky over the Rock River in the city where Reagan — then known as "Dutch" — spent much of his youth.

Jane Gannon, Pat MacNamara, Ila Cannon, and Elwood Schultz, ranging in age from late middle age to quite old, all knew "Dutch."

"He taught me how to swim," Mrs. MacNamara recalled of the former Dixon lifeguard. "He was so nice."

"We used to pronounce his named 'Reegan' then, but now its 'Reygan'," Mrs. Gannon said. "He was always just like the way he was on television in that debate the other night. So relaxed and nice."

Mrs. Cannon said, "His mother was such a nice woman. She used to sing in the choir."

Schultz added, "I used to play football with him in 1928. Maybe we weren't so good, but we won a trophy."

But Nick Johnson of Ohio, Ill., raised a quizzical eyebrow at the celebration.

"I was sitting at one of those booths they had right in the middle of the street eating a bowl of chili," he said. "And I swear 15 people came up to me and asked is 'Reagan going to be here?'

"It was as if they expected Reagan to drop down there on the bandstand from a cloud."

Downtown Dixon was closed to traffic. The flags of every state flapped from the lightposts. Red, white and blue streamers spanned the parking meters.

Every third store was covered with pictures of Reagan. Signs in the store windows read: "You are invited to the White House for dinner — Go Dutch"; "Dutch treat storewide sale. 20 percent off"; "Ronald Reagan special — pants pressed 50 cents a leg, seat free." "Republican cookies—no 'chips' or 'nuts.' " There was "Dutch" apple pie, "Dutch" chocolate ice cream, Grolsch beer from the Netherlands on sale in a local liquor store.

One storefront blasted the strident strains of "We will rally round the flag again," followed by the "Star Spangled Banner." The shop was entirely devoted to Reagan souvenirs and boasted a T-shirt bearing the word "Dutch" as the biggest seller. The shop owner said business began booming last week.

"Reagan to the top and he can't be stopped," the Dixon High School cheerleaders yelled, piling on top of each other in a pyramid. "R-E-A-G-A-N."

Reagan, who was born a few miles away in Tampico, was in California during the celebration. And he had not been in Dixon since just before the Illinois primary in March.

But just after Reagan went over 402 electoral votes at 10:40 p.m., NBC showed a tape made earlier in the evening of the president-elect and his wife phoning the hometown folks who knew him when.

"I wanted to get home to Dixon and Tampico. I've been trying to get phone numbers all evening of the various parties all evening. I'm one of those fellows with two hometowns. I was born in Tampico but grew up in Dixon.

"You don't know how much this evening means to me. I'll do everything in my power to make sure you won't regret it."

Pres. Jimmy Carter waves to supporters at what was suppose to be his victory party. (UPI Photo)

Ronald Reagan's landslide victory was celebrated by thousands of happy Dixonites at the stage of First St. and Hennepin Ave. Tuesday night. Festivities included a torchlight parade and fireworks display. Additional pictures on Page 15.

Telegraph EXTRA edition first newspaper to proclaim victory

Dixon was the focal point of the United States Tuesday evening as native son Ronald Reagan swamped President Jimmy Carter to become the 40th President.

The Dixon Evening Telegraph was the first newspaper in the world to publish Reagan's victory. Reagan was projected the winner at 7:15 p.m. and copies of the extra edition were distributed shortly thereafter.

"Reagan wins Presidency," headlined the four-page extra edition, which contained copy and photos of the evening's events in Dixon. A copy of the extra edition is included in today's edition as a keepsake.

National coverage was given the extra edition as a copy was featured in an interview conducted by NBC Tuesday evening on the stage constructed on First Street.

The eyes of the world focused on Dixon Tuesday evening and as Mayor George Lindquist related Monday evening at the City Council meeting, "tomorrow evening will be an event long remembered in the city."

Lenny Ingrassia, Telegraph managing editor, right, checks first copies of an extra edition printed Tuesday night proclaiming Reagan's presidential victory. Greg Dimmig, press room employee, takes additional papers off the press. The extra edition is included in today's paper. (Telegraph Photo by Suzanne Hanney)

Election '80
Wrap-up of local, state races

Reagan's hometown newspaper, the *Dixon Telegraph*, celebrates his historic election to the White House.

CHAPTER 7

"PLEASE TELL ME YOU'RE REPUBLICANS"

"WHO'S MINDING THE STORE?"

—RWR

The contrasts could not have been sharper. The atmosphere for Jimmy Carter's January 20, 1977, presidential inauguration had been low-key, stripped of the usual pomp and circumstance. In the aftermath of the war in Vietnam and the Watergate scandal, years in which America seemed to lose its way, Carter spoke of returning to a simpler time. Standing on the East Portico of the Capitol (Carter would turn out to be the last president to date to be inaugurated on that historic spot) he cautioned, "We have learned that 'more' is not necessarily 'better,' that even our great nation has its recognized limits, and that we can neither answer all questions nor solve all problems. We cannot afford to do everything, nor can we afford to lack boldness as we meet the future. So, together, in a spirit of individual sacrifice for the

On January 20, 1981, Ronald Reagan was sworn in as the fortieth president of the United States. Though he was just short of his seventieth birthday, Reagan was ready to begin his greatest job.

common good, we must simply do our best." The crucial words and phrases—"limits" and "sacrifice," "cannot afford to do everything" and "simply do our best"—sounded like he was speaking about a country in decline.

When Carter finished his address, he walked down Pennsylvania Avenue to the White House, hand in hand with his wife, Rosalynn, and accompanied by his young daughter, Amy. This simple act, with its Jeffersonian touches, impressed many Americans. Others believed it was the behavior of a president whose overriding message was that America had reached its limits.

HEROIC DREAMS

Exactly four years later, just a few weeks short of his seventieth birthday, Reagan took the oath of office on the majestic West Front of the Capitol, with the National Mall and the Washington Monument facing him. It almost seemed as if the new location had been selected by a Hollywood director to add grandeur to the occasion. Dressed in a charcoal-gray suit, hatless, tall and handsome, Reagan remarked, "Standing here, one faces a magnificent vista, opening up on this city's special beauty and history. At the end of this open mall are those shrines to the giants on whose shoulders we stand."

On the West Front of the Capitol, a majestic setting for the ceremony, Supreme Court Chief Justice Warren Burger swears Reagan in as president.

Always a storyteller, he had a point to make, and he used the country's history to make it. "Directly in front of me, the monument to a monumental man, George Washington, father of our country . . . Off to one side, the stately memorial to Thomas Jefferson . . . And then, beyond the Reflecting Pool, the dignified columns of the Lincoln Memorial." Washington, Jefferson, Lincoln—fabled leaders, national touchstones, and evidence of America's greatness.

America was and is a great nation—of limitless horizons, of sunrises and not sunsets. Driving his point home, Reagan continued, "We have every right to dream heroic dreams. Those who say that we are in a time when there are no heroes just don't know where to look." As far as he was concerned, the heroes of America's history were brave, resourceful pioneers, and the government they fashioned was meant to serve them and to ensure their freedom. "In this present crisis, government is not the solution to our problem," he intoned. He believed that his duty in office was to readjust the relationship between the people and their government—with its massive bureaucracies—in order to ensure maximum freedom. To do so, he promised to cut taxes, reduce the role of the federal government, and replace government meddling and intervention with the energy and creativity of the free market.

As Reagan spoke, rumors had begun to circulate through the crowd. Unconfirmed news reports claimed that Iran was in the process of releasing

As Ronald Reagan delivered his first inaugural address, he stood with his back to the Capitol, facing the Washington Monument and the Lincoln Memorial. History surrounded him.

"And as we renew ourselves here in our own land, we will be seen as having greater strength throughout the world. We will again be the exemplar of freedom and a beacon of hope for those who do not now have freedom.

"To those neighbors and allies who share our freedom, we will strengthen our historic ties and assure them of our support and firm commitment. We will match loyalty with loyalty. We will strive for mutually beneficial relations. We will not use our friendship to impose on their sovereignty, for our own sovereignty is not for sale.

"As for the enemies of freedom, those who are potential adversaries, they will be reminded that peace is the highest aspiration of the American people. We will negotiate for it, sacrifice for it; we will not surrender for it, now or ever."

—*RWR, inaugural address, January 1981*

Reagan speaks to members of Congress and other guests at the traditional Capitol lunch on Inauguration Day, announcing that the fifty-two American hostages in Iran had just been released.

the fifty-two American hostages that they had held for 444 days. Those hostages—and Carter's futile efforts to gain their release or to rescue them—had become the very symbol of the limits America faced overseas. And now, in an act that could have been scripted by a Republican filmmaker, it seemed the national nightmare was about to end.

Shortly after giving his inaugural address, the new president learned that the hostages had been released. At the traditional Capitol lunch with members of Congress and other guests, he announced that the plane carrying the freed Americans had passed across Iranian airspace and was streaking toward friendly lands. Cheers and tears greeted his words, suggesting a scene from *Mr.*

Smith Goes to Washington as much as anything from real life. While Carter had labored tirelessly on the hostages' behalf and had worked out the deal for their release, Reagan accepted the applause and was awarded the credit. It was an auspicious beginning to his presidency.

The Capitol phase of the inauguration concluded, the new president headed for the White House, not on foot but in an open-topped limousine. As he stood, his head and torso visible through the top of the limo, he smiled, clasping his hands above his head like a victorious heavyweight boxer. Beside him, Nancy was dressed flawlessly in a red outfit, crowned by a red hat. The image, so different from Carter's inauguration four years before, was less of a democratic parade than a coronation. The message, again in contrast to Carter, was one of a new beginning.

A NEW BEGINNING

Few realized just how new a beginning it was until the Reagan administration began to govern the country. To begin with, the governing styles of Reagan and Carter were polar opposites. With a finger in every policy pot and a head full of facts and figures, Carter was the quintessential micromanager. He had a long and involved answer for every question. As Reagan had made abundantly clear during his terms as governor of California, he was not the sort of executive who wanted to tramp through the thick weeds of any policy issue. Rather than press conferences, he preferred

The Presidential Inaugural Committee
requests the honor of your presence
to attend and participate in the Inauguration of
Ronald Wilson Reagan
as President of the United States of America
and
George Herbert Walker Bush
as Vice President of the United States of America
on Tuesday the twentieth of January
one thousand nine hundred and eighty one
in the City of Washington

Co-Chairmen
Robert K. Gray
Charles Z. Wick

RONALD WILSON REAGAN

DIXON, IL
JAN
20
1981
61021

INAUGURATION DAY

The Inauguration of the 40th President
January 20, 1981

On February 26, 1981, President Reagan and the First Lady escort British prime minister Margaret Thatcher and Dennis Thatcher to a state dinner, one of many required social duties of the presidency.

scripted comments. Years of film acting had made him proficient at hitting his marks and delivering his lines. His treasury secretary Donald Regan wrote, "Every moment of every public appearance was scheduled, every word scripted, every place where Reagan was supposed to stand was chalked with toe marks."

The president particularly enjoyed the ceremonial aspects of his position. State dinners, visits with dignitaries, delivering speeches, telling stories of his time in Hollywood—these were a few of his favorite things, and were well suited to his personality. Large audiences energized him. Conferences with

Reagan cuts in on Frank Sinatra dancing with Nancy during the president's birthday party in the East Room on February 6, 1981.

small groups of politicians bored him. Even at regular cabinet meetings, he was apt to tune out and drop out of the conversation, leaving subordinates mystified about the direction in which he wanted his administration to move.

Yet on the most important domestic and foreign policy issues—taxes and economic plans, the Cold War and relations with the Soviet Union—he was as sound as a dollar and as square as a brick. He believed with every fiber of his being in the free-market economy and anticommunism, convinced that tax reduction would lead to economic growth and that the Soviet Union was up to no good.

Ronald Reagan walks along the White House colonnade on his way to work.

Jelly beans were a favorite of the president's, and were often offered as a snack during serious discussions among his advisors, including National Security Advisor Richard Allen (far left) and Secretary of State Alexander Haig.

In his inaugural address Reagan had promised action on the economic front, and a few weeks later in a speech to the nation he presented his plan to the American people. The national economy, he began, was in "the worst economic mess since the Great Depression." Increased taxes were not the answer. Before World War II, on average a worker had to labor one month per year to pay his or her taxes; in just over forty years, that ratio had risen to four months per year. Reagan argued that the solution to the country's economic situation was not more taxes, increased bureaucratic red tape, and more government spending, but rather fewer taxes, less federal regulation, and reduced federal expenditures.

Reagan was very clear on the goal of his economic program: "Our aim is to increase our national wealth so all will have more, not just redistribute what we already have, which is just a sharing of scarcity . . . We can leave our children with an unrepayable massive debt and a shattered economy, or we can leave them liberty in a land where every individual has the opportunity to be whatever God intended us to be."

President Reagan and Vice President George H. W. Bush with the cabinet in 1981. Reagan delegated many responsibilities, but he set the tone and direction of his administration.

Supply-side economics—the macroeconomic theory behind his plan—was simple enough in its broad outlines: cut individual and corporate tax rates and roll back government regulations. These actions will lead to an increase in economic freedom and activity, which in turn creates more jobs, higher incomes, greater buying power, and sustained economic growth. In short, supply-side economics provide a better economic life for more people, or the greatest good for the greatest number.

The challenge for Reagan and his administration was selling a plan that demanded a great deal of trust. When he proposed "a 10 percent reduction across the board in personal income tax rates

President Reagan meets with National Security Advisor Richard Allen in the Oval Office. Allen served in the position until early 1982.

Vice President George H. W. Bush and Speaker of the House Thomas "Tip" O'Neill look on as President Reagan addresses a joint session of Congress. Reagan and O'Neill learned to put party politics aside and work together on crucial domestic issues.

On March 30, 1981, President Reagan gave an address to the Building Trades Council of the AFL-CIO at the Washington Hilton Hotel. But the day would not be remembered for anything he said during that speech.

for each of the next three years" and "accelerated depreciation allowances for business," it was clear that the wealthiest Americans, with the highest tax rates, would be showered with the blessings of the plan. Less-wealthy citizens, however, would have to accept on faith that somewhere down the economic road the benefits from this increase in prosperity would trickle down to them. This central idea is what Reagan needed to sell to the American people.

GUNSHOTS AND BLOOD

On the afternoon of March 30, 1981, just sixty-nine days into his term, Reagan had a chance to pitch his program. The Building Trades Council of the

AFL-CIO was in town. If Reagan could convince these representatives of American workers of the viability of his approach, it would put pressure on Democratic legislators to vote with Republicans. Always conscious of even minute details of stage-craft, he replaced his twenty-dollar gold coin Corum watch, a very expensive Swiss production, with an older, more modest timepiece that he normally wore while working on the ranch.

His speech at the Washington Hilton on Connecticut Avenue went well enough and he departed from a side door at 2:25 p.m., moving confidently into the gray mist outside. He acknowledged a cluster of people to his right, and when a few onlookers to his left said, "Mr. President! Mr. President!" he glanced in that direction, waving with his left hand and smiling broadly. At that moment, two shots, followed quickly by four more, exploded like a string of firecrackers.

White House security chief Jerry Parr, who as a child had joined Brass Bancroft's Junior Secret Service Club, hit Reagan like a linebacker, knocking him through the open door of the presidential limousine and covering him with his own body. "Haul ass! Let's get out of here!" Parr instructed the driver, who stepped hard on the pedal and raced down Connecticut Avenue. Somehow in the confusion and swirl of activity, Reagan later recalled seeing a blond man firing a handgun.

"Jerry, get off, I think you've broken one of my ribs," the president said. Then he coughed, bright, frothy blood appearing on his lips. Although there was no visible sign of a bullet wound, something had cut into his lungs, and a moment of crisis suddenly turned much worse.

"Rawhide not hurt," Parr radioed to another car, using the president's code name, hoping to throw off anyone listening in on the Secret Service frequency. "Let's hustle," he continued, giving the other agents a sense of the severity of the situation.

As President Reagan exited the Washington Hilton after his speech, gunman John Hinckley Jr. shot him in the chest. At first, Reagan little suspected the extent of his injuries.

Dear President Reagan,
We hope you get well really soon. We love you. We think you are a good president.

Mrs. Spieler's
Kindergarten class
Phil Swing School
Brawley, Calif.

The American people—including schoolchildren from across the nation—showered President Reagan with get-well cards and messages during his recovery from the attempt on his life.

Get Well Soon

Mr. President

Get
Well
Soon

President
Ronald
Regan

Sincerely
Stacey Saubry
I'm 11 years old

GET WELL SOON
Mr. President
Jim, Tim, and Tom

Knowing that time was of the essence, he redirected the motorcade to George Washington University Hospital.

Reagan's face was white as a sheet when he arrived at the hospital a couple of minutes later, but Parr saw that the president wanted to walk into the hospital, not be carried or wheeled in, and he did not intervene. Once Reagan got inside, he collapsed, a few tortured breaths away from death.

Emergency physicians strapped an oxygen mask over his face. A nurse began to attach a line for transfusions of blood. "Oh-oh, he's been shot," she said. She was right. A bullet fragment had

Emergency surgery saved Reagan's life. Throughout the ordeal, the president retained his humor and optimism. His smile remained strong, even if it took some time for him to fully recover.

knifed through Reagan's chest and cut into his lungs. Bleeding internally, he had lost more than half of his blood.

The trauma unit stabilized his condition and prepped him for surgery. By then he had recovered enough to talk. Remembering a line Jack Dempsey used when he lost the heavyweight championship to Gene Tunney, he told Nancy, "Honey, I forgot to duck." His sense of humor returned with the infusion of fresh blood. As attendants wheeled him into surgery he looked at the team of physicians and quipped, "Please tell me you're Republicans."

If he wasn't fully out of danger, he was on his way.

Reagan was lucky. Others were not. The shooter was John Hinckley Jr., a deranged man in his mid-twenties who had become obsessed with actress Jodie Foster after seeing *Taxi Driver* (1976). His attempt to take Reagan's life had no rational motive. His bullets struck three other dedicated public servants during the attack. Police officer Thomas Delahanty was hit in the neck, Secret Service agent Timothy McCarthy in the chest, and Press Secretary James Brady in the head. The two officers fully recovered from their wounds. Brady remained permanently disabled. His death thirty-three years later was ruled a homicide.

"History admires the wise, but it elevates the brave," observed biographer Edmund Morris. It was unquestionably true of Ronald Reagan. His bravery, poise, and humor in the hour after the attempt on his life were nothing short of extraordinary.

Less than one month after being shot, President Reagan was back on the job, attending a cabinet meeting. He deserved the ovation.

Nor did the assassination attempt keep him out of action for long. Back at the White House, with his approval rating soaring, he continued to push for his tax bill and budget plan. With the Democrats holding a solid majority in the House of Representatives, the president had an uphill battle. He found unlikely but welcome support from a faction of Southern Democrats, dubbed "boll weevils," who supported his economic views. By the end of July, the Reagan administration had enough votes to enact the Economic Recovery Tax Act.

THE REAGAN STYLE

As he had demonstrated during his years as governor of California, Reagan's legislative style was more pragmatic and flexible than his rhetoric. He didn't get the 30 percent he wanted, but he did reduce the highest individual rates from 70 percent to 50 percent, slashed the capital gains tax, and achieved other measures designed to strengthen the international competitiveness of American businesses. A few days later, Congress also approved the president's budget. Just as he had done in California, Reagan showed that he could convert his plans and promises into actions and successes.

In addition, he demonstrated a will to stand firm in difficult situations. When the Professional Air Traffic Controllers Organization (PATCO) declared a strike, Reagan took a hard line. PATCO's action violated a law prohibiting strikes by federal employees in critical industries. All air traffic controllers were federal employees. The president announced that he would fire any controller who did not return to work in forty-eight hours. And he did it. "Dammit," he said, "the law is the law."

Most Americans supported his decisive actions in the PATCO confrontation. Yet the goodwill he had gained after the attempt on his life and during his stand against PATCO did not survive continued economic hard times. He had promised Americans that his economic plans would improve all their lives, not just those of the wealthiest. But this didn't happen immediately. The recession he had inherited from Carter worsened, unemployment crept upward, and the deficit increased.

Reagan's popularity suffered. By November 1982, his approval rating had dipped to 41 percent, and his party took a hit in the midterm elections. The American people's faith in him and in his policies was disappearing. Just two years after his inauguration, his approval rating had gone down to 35 percent. But while others lost hope, Reagan's burned bright in his typical optimistic fashion. "Stay the course," he said. He believed in a better tomorrow.

Tomorrow came sooner than perhaps even he expected. Early in 1983, the economy bottomed out and bounced upward. The reasons for the recovery were as mystifying for most Americans as the Laffer curve, so they just credited it to so-called Reaganomics. Like every president before him, Reagan was delighted to take credit for good economic news. And in a series of foreign policy speeches and successes, he supplied the American people with even more good tidings to crow about.

GAMES AND MEMORIES

And crow they did. In 1984, for instance, Los Angeles hosted the Summer Olympics. The United States had boycotted the 1980 Moscow Olympics because of the Soviet invasion of Afghanistan, and

The 1984 Los Angeles Olympics were a booming success for the American team. Reagan officially opened the games, and later congratulated the U.S. team on its many medals. Smiling beside the president is gymnast Mary Lou Retton, one of the American gold medalists and a darling of the 1984 games.

in 1984 the Soviet Union and its allies returned the insult, boycotting the games in Los Angeles. Spectators were denied the performances of outstanding athletes from the Soviet Union and other communist countries such as Bulgaria, East Germany, Czechoslovakia, Hungary, Poland, and Cuba. But instead of lamenting the diminished competition, Americans cheered as their athletes went for the gold.

The absence of the Soviets and the Eastern Bloc—consistent favorites in women's track and field and swimming, as well as weightlifting, gymnastics, boxing, and wrestling—meant that U.S. athletes were able to win medals in record numbers, an impossible feat when competing against the Soviet Bloc athletes. Altogether, they captured 174 medals, 83 of them gold. Romania, a communist country that did compete in the 1984 games, finished a distant second with 53 medals.

ABC's coverage of the Olympics made the success of the American athletes even more apparent. With 200 hours of TV time to fill, ABC consistently aired medal ceremonies for events won by Americans, but rarely showed any medal ceremonies when athletes from other nations were victorious. Sportswriter Frank Deford captured the

mood of the games: "One night, at the volleyball competition, the public address announcer said he had a medal result. It was in some cycling event. The gold, he said, went to an American, and he gave the cyclist's name. Cheers! USA! USA! The bronze also went to an American, and he gave the name. Cheers! USA! USA! He didn't even mention the silver medalist's name. Foreigner. And so it continued, with Americans cheering on Goliath until the games ended, neither with a bang nor a whimper but with a cry of USA!"

Reagan celebrated America in his own fashion. In June he traveled to Normandy for the fortieth anniversary of D-Day. Although the major

As part of the fortieth anniversary of the June 6, 1944, D-Day invasion, President Reagan gave a moving tribute to the Army Rangers who took Pointe du Hoc, a fortified position on the Normandy coast. It was a speech that underscored the courage of the troops that fought to free Europe.

After his Pointe du Hoc speech, President Reagan and Nancy Reagan visited the Normandy American Cemetery, which sits just above where the Omaha Beach landings took place. They walked among the crosses and remembered the Americans who had made the ultimate sacrifice.

anniversary celebrations were scheduled for the afternoon of June 6, Deputy Chief of Staff Michael Deaver wanted to schedule an important speech for the morning of June 5 so that it would be the lead story on the morning news shows—effectively pushing coverage of the Democratic presidential primary in California to a lesser spot. After some negotiations, the French agreed.

On that misty morning, with a breeze blowing in off the English Channel, Reagan addressed a group of U.S. Army veterans at Pointe du Hoc, where they had engaged in one of D-Day's most violent battles. On June 6, 1944, U.S. Army Rangers had assaulted the fingerlike peninsula of Pointe du Hoc, landing on a sliver of a beach, scrambling to the top of the sheer 130-foot cliffs, and attacking concrete casements and gun pits. D-Day planners knew the position was crucial for observation and believed that German 155-mm guns on the site

commanded the beaches of Utah and Omaha, and had to be neutralized for a successful invasion. Approximately 225 Rangers attacked Pointe du Hoc. After two days of action, 135 had been killed or wounded. But the Americans took the position.

Standing on a windswept promontory, Reagan passionately and eloquently spoke about what the battle meant. Written by Peggy Noonan, the speech was one of his finest. Summoning all his ability as an orator and the dignity of his office, he quietly and modestly described what the Rangers had done. He relayed how they landed and looked up at the Germans, how they shot rope ladders toward the top and struggled up the face, how as one man fell another would take his place. "Soon, one by one, the Rangers pulled themselves over the top—and in seizing the firm land at the top of these cliffs they began to seize back the continent of Europe."

Then, looking into the audience at the men in their sixties and seventies, some infirm, and most graying, Reagan said softly, "These are the boys of Pointe du Hoc. These are the men who took the cliffs. These are the champions who helped free the continent. These are the heroes who helped end a war."

By then many of the Rangers were weeping, as were members of the press corps. Even the Secret Service agents, who should have been scanning the crowd for potential dangers, were listening, and their feelings were evident. Had the speech ended there it would have been a moving tribute. But Reagan continued, adding meaning to the emotions he had aroused.

"You risked everything here," he said to the veterans. "Why? Why did you do it?" Answering his own question, he said, "The men of Normandy had faith that what they were doing was right, faith that they fought for humanity, faith that a just God would grant them mercy on this beachhead or on the next." Who could doubt their faith? "You were here to liberate, not to conquer," Reagan said, adding that what they fought for—their country, democracy, and liberty—were worth the risks they took that day.

Sweeping across forty years to the present, Reagan observed that, sadly, not all of the occupied countries gained liberty. "Soviet troops that came to the center of this continent did not leave

At the fortieth anniversary of the D-Day invasion, President Reagan spoke eloquently about the "boys of Pointe du Hoc," and shook the hands of the men who had returned for the ceremony.

when peace came. They're still there, uninvited, unwanted, unyielding . . . Because of this, allied forces still stand on the continent."

At this point, Reagan reined in his anti-Soviet rhetoric. This was not another "Evil Empire" speech. And if he didn't exactly hold out an olive branch, he came close. "We try always to be prepared for peace; prepared to deter aggression; prepared to negotiate the reduction of arms; and, yes, prepared to reach out again in the spirit of reconciliation. In truth, there is no reconciliation we would welcome more than a reconciliation with the Soviet Union," he affirmed. Little did he realize how those words would echo through the rest of his years in office.

After the Pointe du Hoc speech, he and Nancy visited the American military cemetery at Colleville-sur-Mer, where 9,387 crosses and Stars of David testify to the sacrifices Americans made for liberty. Together they placed a bouquet of red and white carnations and blue irises next to the grave of Brigadier General Theodore Roosevelt Jr., Teddy Roosevelt's son, who led American forces on Utah Beach and died a little more than a month later. Buried beside "Ted" is his brother Quentin, a flier who was killed in aerial combat over France in World War I.

Reagan's speech touched millions of Americans, and the president's popularity soared. In November 1982, after the disastrous midterm elections, it seemed like Reagan was destined to be a one-term president. By June 1984, the upcoming election appeared to be a mere afterthought.

1981–1984
TIMELINE

JANUARY 20, 1981 Reagan is sworn in as fortieth president of the United States. That same day, Iran releases the fifty-two American hostages after 444 days in captivity.

MARCH 30, 1981 After only three months in office, Reagan is shot in the chest by John Hinckley Jr. as he departs the Washington Hilton. Reagan survives the assassination attempt, but the bullet narrowly misses his heart. Hinckley is found not guilty by reason of insanity.

AUGUST 3, 1981 Reagan fires more than 12,000 striking air-traffic controllers after they refuse to return to work within forty-eight hours.

AUGUST 13, 1981 Reagan signs the Economic Recovery Tax Act of 1981 into law, providing a dramatic tax cut for all Americans.

SEPTEMBER 25, 1981 Sandra Day O'Connor is sworn in as first female Supreme Court justice.

1982 A major recession sweeps the nation. Unemployment rates soar. More than nine million Americans are out of work.

MAY 31, 1982 The United States and the Soviet Union announce Strategic Arms Reduction talks.

AUGUST 20, 1982 Reagan's Middle East initiative "Fresh Start" begins.

MARCH 23, 1983 Reagan addresses the nation on National Security and the Strategic Defense Initiative (SDI).

JUNE 5, 1984 Reagan gives a speech at Pointe du Hoc in France for the fortieth anniversary of D-Day.

CHAPTER 8

MORNING IN AMERICA

"I DID TURN 75 TODAY, BUT REMEMBER, THAT'S ONLY 24 CELSIUS."

—*RWR*

Walter Mondale knew it was coming. He could tell from the moment Reagan, standing at the lectern to his right, ducked his head and smiled when *Baltimore Sun* reporter Henry Trewhitt asked about the president's advanced age. The implication behind the question was clear. Is a seventy-three-year-old man up for this job?

Reagan brought his prerehearsed line into his head. Although he muffed the delivery, the blow landed. "I will not make age an issue of this campaign," he said, a sincere, serious look on his face. Then he dropped the other shoe. "I am not going to exploit, for political purposes"—his eyes twinkled for just an instant—"my opponent's youth and inexperience."

The fifty-four-year-old senator from Minnesota laughed—a real laugh, not a stage one—as the audience roared. Reagan had

Chief Justice Warren Burger inaugurates Ronald Reagan as president for the second time while Nancy holds the Bible.

After a limp performance in the first presidential debate, Reagan came back strong in the second debate, held in Kansas City on October 21, 1984, delivering the most memorable line of the entire campaign.

just neutralized the Democrats' most effective line of attack. For all intents and purposes, the 1984 presidential election was over. Reagan drank contentedly from his water glass, giving the crowd time to show its approval.

"Let Ronnie be Ronnie," Nancy had urged Mike Deaver a few days earlier. Reagan's first debate with Mondale had been a disaster. The president seemed weak and confused. Afterward, he complained about having too many facts crammed into his head. People responded to stories and one-liners, he maintained, not detailed policy arguments.

Two weeks after the zinger in Kansas City, Reagan racked up 59 percent of the popular vote on his way to a 525–13 electoral victory. His "Morning in America" slogan—appropriated from Reagan's immensely popular campaign commercial—reflected real improvements since the dismal days of 1980. Inflation was down, largely because of the aggressive actions taken by Fed chairman Paul Volcker in the late 1970s. Unemployment was down too, and the stock market was on the rise. Although many inner-city dwellers, family farmers, and wage laborers were struggling mightily, a new sense of optimism pervaded much of the country.

TROUBLED TIMES

Reagan enjoyed a 62 percent approval rating when he took the oath of office, yet his second term produced more challenges than triumphs.

Nancy hadn't wanted him to run. She dreamed of resuming their comfortable life in California. But Reagan insisted that he had more work to do. As was usually the case, his gentle firmness won her over.

Trouble soon found him. Reagan's 1985 trip to West Germany was supposed to provide a low-stakes opportunity to bolster America's democratic allies while observing the fortieth anniversary of the end of World War II. Instead, it became a fiasco. The president's itinerary had him laying a wreath at Germany's Bitburg military cemetery. Bitburg, it turned out, was the final resting place for forty-nine members of Hitler's notorious SS. Making matters worse, Reagan's visit would coincide with Passover week. "I cannot believe that the president whom I have seen crying at a Holocaust remembrance ceremony would visit a German military cemetery and refuse to visit Dachau," author Elie Wiesel lamented.

Reagan, after much persuasion, adjusted his schedule. He would not back down on visiting Bitburg, but he shifted the venue of his address to the Bergen-Belsen concentration camp, where he

West German chancellor Helmut Kohl follows the Reagans as they walk past the Bergen-Belsen concentration camp memorial.

President Reagan lays a wreath at the Bergen-Belsen concentration camp in northern Germany, where as many as seventy thousand prisoners perished during World War II.

spoke before mass graves containing the remains of fifty thousand Jews. The president blamed the whole kerfuffle on the press.

More bad news came in July, when a routine surgery to remove a polyp from his colon revealed a large mass, probably cancerous. Nancy insisted on telling her husband the news herself. "Does this mean I won't be getting dinner tonight?" he replied after hearing the diagnosis.

Doctors removed the mass on July 14. Reagan's recovery went remarkably well. Within a few days he was reading Westerns and watching old movies. His

trademark optimism withstood the crisis. "I didn't have cancer," he contended. "I had something inside of me that had cancer in it, and it was removed." He wasn't prone to distractions. Once the tumor left his body, it also left his mind. He was even doing some work by July 17. "Some strange soundings are coming from some Iranians," he wrote in his diary that evening. "It could be a breakthrough on getting our seven kidnap victims back."

Reagan's upbeat nature concealed the ravages of cancer—and time. He was slowing down, conserving his faculties for the few issues that really interested him. Although he remained mentally sharp when needed, he fell silent for long periods, as if waiting for someone to cue his next line. He became more dependent on his notecards and seemed baffled whenever someone asked him a question that lacked a scripted answer. He wound down most days by five o'clock and was in pajamas soon after. A *Saturday Night Live* sketch depicting the president as a micromanaging mastermind who spouted statistics, quoted Montesquieu, and spoke fluent Arabic drew big laughs precisely because the country could tell he was slipping.

Facing a divided Congress and increasingly shifting his focus to foreign affairs, Reagan claimed few legislative victories during his second term. Perhaps the most important was the 1986 Tax Reform Act. This overhaul slashed the top tax bracket from 50 percent to 28 percent. It also increased the capital gains tax rate and closed many loopholes that had previously enabled profitable corporations to avoid paying much (if anything) in taxes. Its passage resulted in six million low-income Americans being dropped from the tax rolls altogether. Instead of the supply-side revolution Reagan had promised, the Tax Reform Act represented a modest tax hike that made the overall system a bit fairer and simpler. It again reflected Reagan's pragmatism; on the same day he signed the bill, the Treasury Department announced a $220.7 billion budget deficit for 1986, at that time the largest in American history. The president understood that the federal government could not balance the budget solely with spending cuts, and that lower tax rates did not necessarily boost revenues.

Reagan signs the 1986 Tax Reform Act.

Overall view of the signing ceremony for the 1986 Tax Reform Act on the South Lawn of the White House. Reagan realized that his earlier tax cuts had reduced revenues too much. The bill represented a careful, pragmatic compromise between liberal and conservative priorities. While cutting the tax rate paid by millionaires, it also closed loopholes and freed many low-income Americans from paying federal income taxes. On the whole it created a more progressive tax system that increased revenues.

THE GREAT COMMUNICATOR

Successful presidents are more than executive bureaucrats who organize departments and sign bills into law. They also serve as national father figures who guide the American people through tough times. For Reagan, this was never more true than on January 28, 1986. His staff was working hard on an important speech, as the president's State of the Union address was scheduled for that evening. Besides laying out the president's agenda for the coming year, the speech would include his first mention of the word "AIDS."

Few people in the White House were paying attention to the day's other big story. Space shuttle launches had become routine since *Columbia* made its inaugural flight in 1981. While Reagan's speech-writers were busy with their final efforts on the State of the Union speech, Mission Control was counting down the seconds before the space shuttle *Challenger* lifted off for the fleet's twenty-fifth mission.

Then, disaster. A faulty seal in one of its boosters gave way, causing an explosion that killed all seven members of its crew, including a civilian teacher, Christa McAuliffe. All activity in the West

On January 28, 1986, the space shuttle *Challenger*, with seven astronauts on board—including the first civilian in space, teacher Christa McAuliffe—exploded just seventy-four seconds after takeoff, on live television.

"Today is a day for mourning and remembering. Nancy and I are pained to the core by the tragedy of the shuttle *Challenger*. We know we share this pain with all of the people of our country. This is truly a national loss . . . We mourn seven heroes: Michael Smith, Dick Scobee, Judith Resnik, Ronald McNair, Ellison Onizuka, Gregory Jarvis, and Christa McAuliffe. We mourn their loss as a nation together.

"For the families of the seven . . . your loved ones were daring and brave, and they had that special grace, that special spirit that says, 'Give me a challenge, and I'll meet it with joy.' They had a hunger to explore the universe and discover its truths. They wished to serve, and they did. They served all of us. We've grown used to wonders in this century. It's hard to dazzle us. But for twenty-five years the United States space program has been doing just that . . . We're still pioneers. They, the members of the *Challenger* crew, were pioneers.

"And I want to say something to the schoolchildren of America who were watching the live coverage of the shuttle's takeoff. I know it is hard to understand, but sometimes painful things like this happen . . . It's all part of taking a chance and expanding man's horizons. The future doesn't belong to the fainthearted; it belongs to the brave. The *Challenger* crew was pulling us into the future, and we'll continue to follow them . . . We will never forget them, nor the last time we saw them, this morning, as they prepared for their journey and waved good-bye and 'slipped the surly bonds of earth' to 'touch the face of God.'"

—*RWR, Presidential address, January 28, 1986*

Reagan's heartfelt Oval Office address following the *Challenger* explosion offered one of the country's great moments in presidential rhetoric.

Reagan, along with (left to right) Deputy White House Press Secretary Larry Speakes, Presidential Assistant Dennis Thomas, Special Assistant Jim Kuhn, Communications Director Pat Buchanan, and Chief of Staff Donald Regan, watches a replay of one of the most horrifying moments ever presented on live television: the explosion of the space shuttle *Challenger*.

Wing halted. Reagan cradled his head in his right hand as he stared at the television, thinking of the families who had just lost loved ones and of the children who were seeing the same horrific pictures in their schools.

His devoted speechwriter Peggy Noonan translated his initial thoughts into a brief, wistful soliloquy that contextualized the tragedy as an unfortunate, inescapable consequence of man's insatiable desire to explore unknown realms.

Her draft concluded with a stirring memorial. "We will never forget them, nor the last time we saw them," it read, "as they prepared for their journey and waved good-bye and slipped the surly bonds of earth to touch the face of God." Those final lines came from the poem, "High Flight," by John Gillespie Magee Jr., an American who died flying for the Royal Canadian Air Force a few days after Pearl Harbor. Reagan knew the poem well; his friend Tyrone Power had carried it with him through the war.

Reagan spoke for less than five minutes that evening, looking just as shattered as the rest of the country. His heartfelt address struck a perfect balance of sorrow and hope. While mourning the dead, he assured the world that the United States would keep exploring the heavens. It would not abandon its pioneering spirit in the face of evident risk. Space travel would continue. It was what Americans did.

Reagan delivers his remarks on "Liberty Weekend," a celebration of the hundredth birthday of the Statue of Liberty. With his trademark charm and charisma, the president delivered a patriotic tribute to America's past and offered optimism for the future in the shadow of Lady Liberty.

He again achieved oratorical brilliance five months later, under happier circumstances. The Statue of Liberty's hundredth birthday offered a quintessential Reagan moment. The rededication of an American icon after years of restoration seemed like a metaphor for his entire political philosophy. His July 3, 1986, remarks at the four-day event's opening ceremony again captured the magical combination of charm, erudition, and wonder that defined the president's public persona.

Details rarely interested Reagan, who much preferred painting a big picture for others to admire. On that lovely evening, with Lady Liberty's darkened torch soaring above his head, he created a masterpiece.

His words might have sounded cloying had he not believed them with all his heart. "Call it mysticism if you will," he said, "but I have always believed there was some divine providence that placed this great land here between the two great oceans, to be found by a special kind of people from every corner of the world, who had a special love for freedom and a special courage that enabled them to leave their own land, leave their friends and countrymen, and come to this new and strange land to build a New World of peace and freedom and hope."

But the statue (only Reagan could have gotten away with calling it "everybody's gal") represented more than American exceptionalism. It also symbolized one generation's promise to the next, a passing of the torch that, in his mind, began with the Pilgrims and extended to the present day. "We're bound together," he reminded the audience, "because, like them, we dare to hope—hope that our children will always find here the land of liberty in a land that is free. We dare to hope too that we'll understand our work can never be truly done until every man, woman, and child shares in our gift, in our hope, and stands with us in the light of liberty—the light that, tonight, will shortly cast its glow upon her, as it has upon us for two centuries, keeping faith with a dream of long ago and guiding millions still to a future of peace and freedom."

The speech captured in words Reagan's love for America. His "America" was without a doubt more perfect than the real thing. For the most part it lacked poverty, racism, and other social ills. It never acted questionably overseas. Reagan's "America," as his *Challenger* and Statue of Liberty speeches made abundantly clear, was really more of a promise and a set of principles than a location. Striving, pioneering, independent, free, optimistic—that had always been his "America," regardless of the circumstances in reality. That relentless idealism gave Reagan his appeal. How could critics drag down someone who simply would not pull his head out of the clouds?

Those two pitch-perfect moments, one born of tragedy and the other of celebration, provided some of the final high spots of Reagan's administration. As happens to many presidents, his final few years in office often wavered between anticlimactic and downright awful.

OVERSEAS PROBLEMS

November 1986 brought unwelcome political news. After the election, Democrats not only expanded their majority in the House, but also took control of the Senate. This development made passing legislation more difficult. In addition, two intertwined foreign operations threatened to do far greater damage.

Reagan was a firm believer in the domino theory, the Cold War principle that holds that a successful communist movement in one country will imperil neighboring territories. If left unchecked, communism's gravitational pull could send an entire row of nations toppling into the Soviet camp.

He saw an emerging threat in Central America, where leftist movements in El Salvador and Nicaragua were battling American-backed anti-communist forces. The thought of communism marching toward Texas was too much for Reagan, who had been pumping resources into the right-wing opposition campaigns since the opening months of his presidency.

In Nicaragua, that meant supporting the Contras' fight against the ruling Sandinistas. Reagan considered the Contras "the moral equivalent of our Founding Fathers" despite their unpopularity within Nicaragua and their reputation for brutality. Millions of dollars in covert funds

National Security Council staffer Lieutenant Colonel Oliver North (center) and President Reagan share a light moment with Contra leader Adolfo Calero.

Reagan discusses his remarks on the Iran-Contra Affair with (left to right) Secretary of Defense Caspar Weinberger, Secretary of State George Shultz, Attorney General Ed Meese, and Chief of Staff Don Regan.

flowed south. The CIA recruited and trained resistance fighters at American-funded secret bases in Honduras, Nicaragua's neighbor to the north.

Most congressmen knew nothing about the Contra program until news outlets started leaking the story in late 1982. Passed that same year, the Boland Amendment limited assistance to the Contras and forbade the CIA from using federal money to try to overthrow the Sandinistas. Aid continued nevertheless. Reagan saw the Contra-Sandinista conflict as a straightforward question of good versus evil. He genuinely believed that a communist—or even leftist—Nicaragua posed a direct threat to the United States. Congress passed a second, tougher Boland Amendment in 1984 after

administration officials ignored their promise to update legislators on their covert activities in Latin America. This time, Congress barred any federal agency from "supporting, directly or indirectly, military and paramilitary operations in Nicaragua by any nation, group, organization or individual."

Reagan signed the bill, yet still believed that it did not apply to him or his inner circle. "Congress has eroded away much of the [constitutional] authority of the presidency in foreign affairs," he grumbled in his diary. "They can't and don't have the information the [president] has and they are really lousing things up."

"I want you to do whatever you have to do to help [the Contras] keep body and soul together,"

Reagan told National Security Advisor Robert McFarlane soon after Congress enacted the second Boland Amendment. McFarlane, along with National Security Council staffer Lieutenant Colonel Oliver North, began raising funds from Israel, Saudi Arabia, South Africa, and other friendly nations, as well as from wealthy sympathizers such as beer mogul Joseph Coors. A shady network of arms dealers, drug smugglers, and soldiers of fortune, known collectively as the Enterprise, funneled illicit cash and equipment toward the Contras. Although Reagan may not have known the particulars, he was certainly aware of the program.

The Enterprise eventually merged its Contra operation with another secret, illegal venture. Terrorists in Lebanon took seven Americans hostage in mid-1985. In addition to his intense desire to secure the captives' release, Reagan understood the political toll an event like this could take. He had, after all, campaigned for president during the Iran hostage crisis. He desperately wanted to free them but had no real leverage for doing so. His pledge that "Americans will never make concessions with terrorists" limited his range of options.

Back-channel messages from the Israelis suggested a way out. Iran, immersed in a life-or-death struggle with its rival Iraq, badly needed weapons. Israeli intelligence suggested that a group of Iranian moderates, opponents of the Ayatollah Khomeini's regime, were willing to exert pressure on Lebanon in exchange for American firepower. To conceal

1985–1988 TIMELINE

JANUARY 20, 1985 Reagan is sworn in for his second term at seventy-three, making him the oldest president to take the oath of office.

MAY 5, 1985 The president visits Bitburg military cemetery and the Bergen-Belsen concentration camp.

JUNE 14, 1985 TWA flight 847 is hijacked by Lebanese terrorists. Thirty-nine hostages are taken and held in Beirut.

JULY 13, 1985 Reagan is admitted to Bethesda Navy Medical Center for colon cancer surgery.

NOVEMBER 17, 1985 Lt. Col. Oliver North negotiates the shipment of antiaircraft missiles to Iran.

JANUARY 28, 1986 The space shuttle *Challenger* explodes seventy-four seconds after takeoff, killing all aboard.

JUNE 25, 1986 Congress approves the president's request for aid to the Contras in Nicaragua by just twelve votes.

OCTOBER 1986 Congress enacts Reagan's 1986 Tax Reform Act, which reduces the top tax rate from 50% to 28%.

NOVEMBER 25, 1986 Attorney General Edwin Meese reports that thirty million dollars of profits from arms sales to Iran were used to fund Contra rebels.

DECEMBER 2, 1986 Reagan's approval rating plunges from 67% to 46% in the aftermath of the Iran-Contra affair.

MARCH 4, 1987 Following the Tower Commission report on the Iran-Contra affair, Reagan addresses the nation, admitting his staff misled him.

OCTOBER 17, 1987 Nancy Reagan undergoes breast cancer surgery.

JUNE 1988 The U.S. unemployment rate reaches a fourteen-year low.

Reagan feels the weight of the Tower Commission report, which detailed the many crimes involved in the Iran-Contra scandal. The commission, which Reagan personally appointed, said the president's hands-off managerial style paved the way for the illegalities.

the trade, Israel would provide the weapons from its own arsenal, which the Americans would then replenish. Reagan authorized the program while recovering from his July 1985 cancer surgery. Considering the circumstances, he may not have been in the most lucid frame of mind.

Hundreds of missiles traveled from Israel to Iran over the next several months. Reagan reauthorized the transfers in December 1985 even as the CIA warned that the shipments would neither free the hostages nor empower the Iranian opposition enough to destabilize Khomeini's regime.

In early 1986, Lieutenant Colonel North hit on the "neat idea" of redirecting profits from Iranian weapon sales to the Contras. Reagan was probably unaware of this linkage even though he knew about its constituent parts. The Enterprise's network gained new life at the very moment when the president signed a law forbidding arms sales to terrorist nations, a list that specifically included Iran. Missile sales continued even after North and McFarlane realized that their Iranian contacts had little influence over the hostage takers.

A November 1986 exposé in a Lebanese magazine revealed what became known as the Iran-Contra affair. Reagan denied any knowledge of the diversion of funds to Nicaragua. This was likely true, but his statement ignored what he *did* know, and it downplayed the illegal activities occurring within his administration.

Reagan never really accepted that he had broken multiple laws. Iran-Contra didn't *feel* wrong to him. How, he wondered, could fighting communists and trying to free hostages be crimes? The American people, on the other hand, made their displeasure known. They could not understand why Reagan sold weapons to a country that had taken American hostages of its own several years earlier. The president's approval ratings quickly tumbled from 63 percent to 36 percent. Revelations that Oliver North had shredded key documents undermined the country's faith in the government. Talk of impeachment rumbled around Washington. Perhaps worst of all, Lebanon had freed only three of the hostages while taking three more.

Lieutenant Colonel Oliver North's defiant testimony before the House Foreign Relations Committee made him an unlikely hero in some quarters.

Reagan meeting with members of the Tower Commission in 1987. The Iran-Contra affair occupied much of the president's time during 1986 and 1987. The mounting crisis devastated his approval ratings and undercut his political effectiveness.

A TOUGH FINAL YEAR

Iran-Contra dogged Reagan throughout 1986 and 1987. Congressional hearings on the scandal were held in the summer of 1987 and uncovered many of the affair's unseemly details. Fortunately for Reagan, the economy was humming along and few people had the stomach for another impeachment drama just a dozen years after President Richard Nixon resigned under the cloud of Watergate.

The Iran-Contra story was dissipating by the fall of 1987, when Reagan absorbed several new blows. On October 19, the stock market plummeted 508 points, losing 22.6 percent of its value. "I don't know what meaning it might have," Reagan conceded. Although rapid action by the Federal Reserve stemmed the panic, many blamed the president for the downturn.

Reagan took another hit four days later when the Senate rejected Robert Bork's nomination for the Supreme Court by a 58–42 vote, the widest margin of defeat for any nominee in history. Bork was a brilliant, if rigid, conservative jurist with a gift for rubbing people the wrong way. He had tacked to the center during his acrimonious hearings, an ideological shift that ended up undermining his credibility. Reagan next proposed the more moderate Douglas Ginsburg, who quickly withdrew after admitting occasional marijuana use during the 1960s and 1970s—a symbolic no-no for the "Just Say No" era. "It's about time for Ronald

Finally some good news for Reagan as Nancy comes home from the hospital after a mastectomy. The First Lady dismissed accusations that she was overreacting to her diagnosis and became a powerful voice for breast cancer screening and treatment.

Reagan to take charge of his White House," conservative senator Orrin Hatch grumbled. Anthony Kennedy, Reagan's third nominee, eventually filled the open seat.

October 1987 also brought personal disaster. John Hutton, the White House physician, was waiting when the president exited a cabinet meeting on the fifth. "I'm afraid I have rather bad news regarding the First Lady's mammogram," he said. Reagan sat stone-faced behind his desk. "Well, you're doctors, and I'm confident you'll be able to take care of it," he replied.

The president was much less stoic the next day when doctors at Bethesda Naval Hospital confirmed that Nancy had a tumor, probably malignant, in her left breast. He disintegrated, sobbing in a nurse's arms in a private room.

The Reagans were terrified. Nancy opted for a mastectomy rather than a lumpectomy. She worried about her husband's reaction to the operation but felt it was the only way to be certain the cancer was gone. The couple kept the news private for ten days, informing the press only on the day of Nancy's procedure. They kept the children in the dark too. Doria, Ron Jr.'s wife, had been told, but Nancy didn't want to alarm the others. She informed them through an aide just before reporters got the story.

After the operation, Nancy opened her eyes to see her husband waiting for her, his own eyes gritty with dried tears. "They took my breast," she muttered through a postoperative haze. "I feel so sorry for you."

"Honey, I know you don't feel like dancing, so let's just hold hands," Ronnie replied.

"Please don't let Bob Woodward in my room," Nancy answered, as if the investigative journalist who helped break Watergate were lurking under her bed.

Nancy's full and exceptionally rapid recovery coincided with some of the worst weeks of Reagan's presidency. "Poor Ronnie," she lamented on October 19. "What a week for him! Me, Iran, and now the stock market."

Nancy's returning health buoyed Reagan through these hard times. Then, in another cruel blow, her mother suffered a fatal stroke on October 26. October 1987 had truly been, as she called it in her autobiography, "A Terrible Month."

Reagan's approval ratings crept back over the 50 percent mark in 1988, his final year in the White House. That November he gave America another in a long line of iconic moments. Photographers snapped one of the lasting images of his administration at Governor's Island, about a mile west of the Statue of Liberty. Reagan stands with "everybody's gal" over his left shoulder, pointing into the distance while the president-elect, George H. W. Bush, listens on. It would have been a routine photo, the kind of passing-of-the-torch shot expected of any chief executive, if not for the presence of a most unusual third party. To Reagan's right, gazing together with him into some remote and uncertain distance, stands the general secretary of the Communist Party of the Soviet Union, Mikhail Gorbachev.

CHAPTER 9

REAGAN AND THE RUSSIANS

"FREEDOM AND DEMOCRACY . . . WILL LEAVE MARXISM AND LENINISM ON THE ASH HEAP OF HISTORY."

—RWR

How can I make peace if they keep dying on me?" Reagan asked in March 1985. Konstantin Chernenko, the wheezing, gray eminence who led the Soviet Union for only thirteen months, had just died. With Leonid Brezhnev and Yuri Andropov already gone, President Reagan had now outlasted three Soviet general secretaries. The communists had a knack for selecting leaders who made their American counterpart seem youthful and spry in comparison.

Considering Reagan's long history of dedicated anticommunism, it's remarkable that he could ask such a question. In a speech to the National Association of Evangelicals just two years earlier, he had tarred the Soviet Union as "the focus of evil in the modern world."

Mikhail Gorbachev's relationship with Reagan changed the world forever. George H. W. Bush was left to negotiate his way through the consequences of their actions.

A RED-BAITING PAST

As a private citizen, public speaker, and political candidate, Reagan was free to be an ideological purist. As president, however, he evolved into a pragmatist capable of looking beyond distinctions of right and wrong in order to advance in a desired direction. His critics downplayed this character trait, which had defined both his two terms as governor and his approach toward taxes and other domestic issues while in the White House. His self-confidence and his serene conviction that God would make everything all right in the end enabled him to accept compromises that a more rigid leader would have rejected out of hand.

No one could accuse the president of being soft on Reds. By the late 1940s, in the early days of the Cold War, he had emerged as one of the film industry's loudest anticommunists. "The Communist plan for Hollywood was remarkably simple," he wrote. "It was merely to take over the motion picture business . . . for a grand world-wide propaganda base." His talks for General Electric incorporated anti-Soviet diatribes and dire warnings of creeping socialism at home. His newspaper columns continued these themes through the 1960s and 1970s. Although careful not to personally criticize fellow Republicans, he attacked the Richard Nixon–Henry Kissinger policy of détente with the Soviets as a "one-way street." He insisted that the Russians would never negotiate in good faith because "they reserve unto themselves the right to commit any crime, to lie, to cheat," in order to advance their selfish goals.

Reagan's hard-line stance solidified during his years as an unannounced, then official, presidential candidate. "Communism is neither an economic or a political system," he said in 1975, "it is a form of insanity—a temporary aberration which will one day disappear from the earth because it is contrary to human nature." During the 1980 campaign, he predicted that the Soviet Union would soon go bankrupt.

While anticipating the USSR's demise, Reagan painted a menacing picture of a still-dangerous adversary. He insisted (inaccurately) that the Soviets were spending far more on their military than the Americans. In 1977 he claimed, again wrongly, that the Russians "have a laser beam capable of blasting our missiles from the sky if we should ever use them." While campaigning in 1980, he pointed to their recent invasion of Afghanistan as evidence that communism remained an imminent threat.

HEATING UP THE COLD WAR

Once elected, Reagan accelerated the military buildup begun under his predecessor, Jimmy Carter. He supplied covert aid to anticommunist movements in Afghanistan, El Salvador, and Nicaragua. At the same time, he reached out to the aging Leonid Brezhnev. The two had met briefly in 1973, and the president hoped to build on this tenuous connection. In 1981 he wrote a letter inviting the Russian leader to participate in a "meaningful and constructive dialogue which will assist us in fulfilling our joint obligation to finding lasting peace."

President Reagan continued his predecessor Jimmy Carter's expansion of the military. Reagan reviews the troops as part of the recommissioning ceremony for the USS *New Jersey*.

Brezhnev died in 1982 without ever sitting down with Reagan. His successor, former KGB chairman Yuri Andropov, seemed even less likely to accept Reagan's entreaties. In fact, kidney troubles kept Andropov in the hospital for much of his administration.

Soviet-American relations deteriorated throughout Reagan's first term. The president's harsh rhetoric and lavish spending on nuclear-capable missiles and heavy bombers prompted fears that he was hungry to start World War III. His 1983 green-lighting of the Strategic Defense Initiative (SDI), an ambitious system of missile-destroying satellites and lasers far beyond America's technological

capabilities, convinced the Soviets that he wanted to weaponize outer space. The United States' October 1983 invasion of Grenada after a leftist group seized control of that tiny Caribbean island reinforced images of a militaristic administration flexing its muscles. Around the same time, a Soviet fighter pilot shot down a Korean Airlines jet that had strayed off course, killing 269 people. "My God, have they gone mad?" Reagan asked. Then, in November 1983, NATO launched a military exercise called Able Archer designed to simulate a nuclear attack. Panicked Soviet officials put their forces on alert, fearing that the simulation was actually a real offensive.

THE WHITE HOUSE
WASHINGTON

June 17, 1983

Dear Mr. President:

Please accept my congratulations upon your
election as Chairman of the Presidium of the
Supreme Soviet of the Union of Soviet Socialist
Republics.

As you assume your new duties, I hope that
together we can find ways to promote peace by
reducing the levels of armaments and moving toward
the elimination of force and threats of force in
settling international disputes. You will have my
full cooperation in moving toward these goals on a
basis of equality, reciprocity, and respect for
the rights and interests of all.

Sincerely,

Ronald Reagan

His Excellency
Yuri Vladimirovich Andropov
Chairman, Presidium of the Supreme
        Soviet of the Union of Soviet
        Socialist Republics
Moscow

Reagan's letter to Yuri Andropov
congratulating him on becoming
Soviet president.

Reagan writes to Mikhail Gorbachev
in anticipation of the December 1987
summit in Washington, D.C.

3

THE WHITE HOUSE
WASHINGTON

September 16, 1987

Dear Mr. General Secretary:

It was a great pleasure for me to receive
personal greetings from you and Mrs. Gorbachev
yesterday. Nancy and I appreciate your thought-
fulness.

At the signing of the Agreement on Nuclear Risk
Reduction Centers, I said that I look forward
to the day when you and I can come together to
sign even more historic agreements in our
common search for peace. My meeting yesterday
with Foreign Minister Shevardnadze and his
delegation was a constructive and useful step
in that direction.

Nancy and I wish to take this opportunity to
convey to you and Mrs. Gorbachev our personal
best wishes and our hope that the coming months
will see further steps toward our common goals.

Sincerely,

Ronald Reagan

His Excellency
Mikhail Sergeyevich Gorbachev
General Secretary of the Central Committee
 of the Communist Party of the Soviet Union
The Kremlin
Moscow

The sudden escalation of Cold War tensions rattled Reagan, who realized that the superpower rivalry was in danger of getting out of control. "Maybe I should go see Andropov and propose eliminating all nuclear weapons," he suggested to George Shultz, his secretary of state.

A few days before initiating the Grenada operation, Reagan watched an advance screening of *The Day After*, a made-for-TV movie depicting the impact of a nuclear war on the heartland town of Lawrence, Kansas. It's a brutal film, and one that threw Reagan into a dark mood. "It's very effective & left me greatly depressed," he confided in his diary. "A nuclear war can never be won and must

never be fought," he remarked soon after. "I know I speak for people everywhere when I say our dream is to see the day when nuclear weapons will be banished from the face of the earth."

Reagan was ready to pivot from deterrence to arms reduction, but the Soviets distrusted the man who, in their eyes, had pushed them to the brink of oblivion. Andropov, largely confined to a hospital room, rebuffed his overtures. "I don't want to honor that prick," an uncharacteristically blunt Reagan spat when the Soviet leader died in February 1984. The president skipped the funeral. Andropov's successor, Chernenko, who could barely stand without assistance, also lacked the vision and the energy to

Reagan reviews national defense policy with senior advisor Donald Rumsfeld and Secretary of State George Shultz as Operation Able Archer nearly provokes the Soviets into starting a nuclear war.

respond to the conciliatory messages coming from Washington. Reagan grudgingly consented to sign a condolence book at the Soviet embassy when this latest in a line of geriatric Soviet premiers died.

For all his talk of peace, Reagan's anticommunist reputation still lent weight to his pronouncements, even when offered in jest. In a moment of poor judgment, he opened one 1984 radio address with: "My fellow Americans, I am pleased to tell you I just signed legislation which outlaws Russia forever. The bombing will begin in five minutes." Part of the Soviet army went on alert because the president had not realized he was speaking into a live microphone.

A NEW PARTNER

Following Chernenko's death, Mikhail Gorbachev, a fifty-four-year-old former agriculture secretary, became the Soviet Union's eighth general secretary. "I like Mr. Gorbachev," British prime minister Margaret Thatcher told Reagan. "We can do business with him." Gorbachev accepted what few of his countrymen were willing even to consider: The Soviet Union was in big trouble. Soviet technology, particularly its computers, lagged far behind the technology of the West. The war in Afghanistan was undercutting morale in its military. Its food production and distribution systems were horribly mismanaged. Its industrial base dated from

Reagan signed a condolence book after Soviet premier Yuri Andropov's death, but he felt no great loss. Reagan's first term featured deteriorating relationships with the world's other superpower.

Future Soviet general secretary Mikhail Gorbachev shakes hands with British prime minister Margaret Thatcher in 1984. Thatcher's husband, Dennis, shares a smile with Raisa Gorbachev. The Iron Lady would soon be urging her American counterpart to work with Gorbachev.

the Stalin era. Its leadership had grown stale and entrenched, more intent on maintaining its own power than on delivering services to its citizens.

Gorbachev recognized the need for reform. His top priority was reducing military spending, which consumed a vast percentage of the nation's finances and resources. Bureaucratic inertia, institutionalized paranoia, and general incompetence had allowed the Soviet war machine to metastasize. The Carter-Reagan military buildup had made a bad situation worse by forcing the Russians to spend more to keep from falling even further behind.

At Chernenko's funeral, Vice President George Bush delivered a friendly message from Reagan to the new leader. "I would like you to visit me in Washington at your earliest convenient opportunity," it read.

"I have a positive attitude to the idea you expressed," Gorbachev replied a few weeks later.

More letters bounced between the capitals while Gorbachev slowly wrenched the ponderous Soviet empire in new directions. He called for an end to nuclear testing and hinted at his willingness to reduce nuclear stockpiles. In 1985, while Reagan's handlers were flailing for a way out of the Bitburg mess, Gorbachev was announcing a new policy of perestroika, or economic restructuring, which would introduce elements of the free market and private property into the communist system. Soviet citizens were also—albeit tentatively—embracing glasnost, a new tolerance of dissent. These reforms came not from a love of democracy, but rather from Gorbachev's conviction that communism must change in order to survive. It needed to experiment, to become more nimble, and to consider fresh answers to problems that the political elite barely knew existed.

Reagan was not entirely sure what to make of all this. "I believe Gorbachev is a highly intelligent leader, totally dedicated to traditional Soviet goals," he jotted in a note. He had railed against communism for so long that he could not help but remain suspicious. He suspected that the Russian was playing a long con, laying traps that would ensnare him in an unbalanced arms deal or some public-relations snafu. Perhaps Gorbachev's talk of peace was a trick to throw the Americans on the defensive, or to drive a wedge between the United States and its European allies. Such talk certainly did nothing to diminish American support for the Contras and other anticommunist movements.

A HISTORIC MEETING

After months of maneuverings, Reagan and Gorbachev scheduled a November 1985 meeting in Geneva, Switzerland. Reagan endured hours of presummit briefings. He watched every scrap of videotape of his adversary he could find. He talked strategy with Richard Nixon. He even watched Soviet films, hoping for some insight or edge.

"Lord, I hope I'm ready and not overtrained," he wrote in his diary the night before the leaders met. His fear of overpreparation echoed his frustration following his disastrous first debate against Walter Mondale.

November 19 was a gray, bitterly cold morning. Reagan's problems went beyond the weather. The family that had offered their villa for his stay had left explicit instructions on caring for their young son's fish. As the president prepared for his meeting, he noticed that one of the fish was dead. It was not an auspicious omen.

Gorbachev had won the first round of the public-relations battle a few days earlier by calling for a 50 percent cut in offensive nuclear weapons. Reagan took the second round when he sprang from his villa on that chilly morning without a coat or hat. Gorbachev was heavily bundled, giving him a less-vibrant appearance than the American president. It was a trivial matter, but such visuals often formed the basis of global opinion, as Reagan well knew.

"Don't be nervous," journalist Sam Donaldson shouted. Reagan looked anything but. Gorbachev, a tight smile frozen on his face, looked pensive as the two entered the Villa Pometta. They posed for a few photos while waving off questions from the assembled press. Gorbachev looked disapprovingly at a young man in blue jeans and red high-top sneakers claiming to represent *Playboy* magazine. The Russian probably didn't recognize him as Ronald Reagan Jr.

Once the doors closed, they could begin the serious business of making formal statements. Reagan delivered a canned speech about trust. Gorbachev responded with calls for greater understanding and a stronger commitment to arms control.

Both men were taking the other's measure. Reagan perked up at Gorbachev's frequent references to God, perhaps dropped intentionally to capture the president's interest. He found himself liking the general secretary despite his suspicions. Gorbachev bristled at Reagan's one-sided view of recent history but found him more alert and forceful than he had expected, at least when the conversation concerned subjects that interested him.

That first session went much longer than scheduled. So did that afternoon's gathering. Then, in one of those carefully planned spontaneous moments that characterize politics in the age of television, Reagan invited Gorbachev to join him in the pool house for an informal conversation. Cold lake air turned their breath to steam. Gorbachev told Reagan that he had seen some of his films. He liked them, he remarked, "particularly the one where you lost your legs." Reagan blushed. *Kings*

Reagan and Gorbachev pose for some press-friendly moments at Geneva. The real work of the conference occurred out of sight of the cameras.

Row had been voted one of the ten best movies of all time, he said.

A roaring fire awaited them. Settling into comfortable chairs, they read each other's proposals to mothball weapons systems. Gorbachev balked at SDI, which he insisted would boost the arms race. Reagan, baffled by the Russian's objections, maintained that SDI had no offensive purpose.

Even with their disagreements, they felt a real connection. "I'd like to invite you and Mrs. Gorbachev to visit us in Washington next year," Reagan offered as they parted for the evening. "Yes, after that you must come to Moscow," Gorbachev replied through his interpreter.

"You could almost get to like the guy," Reagan told his advisors. "I keep telling myself I mustn't do it."

Nancy Reagan did not share her husband's ambivalence. "My fundamental impression of Raisa Gorbachev was that she never stopped talking," Nancy complained after her obligatory tea with the Russian first lady. Mrs. Gorbachev's brusque

Surrounded by advisors, two heads of state hash out thorny issues of war and peace. Reagan and Gorbachev had a difficult time connecting until after they escaped from their handlers and were able to meet privately.

Protocol demanded that Nancy have tea with Raisa Gorbachev. Their conversation was strained, to say the least. Nancy found her counterpart rude and unbearable.

demeanor horrified her. She hectored her KGB guards and lectured Mrs. Reagan about the glories of communism. "The conversation was dry, impersonal, and tedious," Nancy recalled. She gritted her teeth throughout the diplomatic niceties.

Reagan and Gorbachev reconvened the following day, this time at the Soviet Mission. Ironically, the atmosphere was tenser than during the previous day's meetings. Reagan decried Russia's poor treatment of Jews. Gorbachev suggested that African Americans fared even worse. With tempers flaring, the Russian again denounced SDI as a precursor to a space-based weapon system.

Angry as they were, both men kept talking.

Their one-on-one became a kind of cathartic experience, an opportunity to air their grievances and move on. "This has been a good meeting," Reagan informed speechwriter Pat Buchanan. "I think I can work with this guy. I can't just keep poking him in the eye."

The Geneva summit produced few concrete results. Beneath that inconclusive surface, however, lay indications of future progress. Both executives had publicly discussed massive cuts in their nuclear arsenals. "I bet the hard-liners in both our countries are bleeding while we shake hands," Reagan whispered to Gorbachev at the closing photo op. Reagan had moved closer to his goal of a nuclear-free world. Gorbachev had shown the entrenched Soviet bureaucracy that his internal reforms had a good chance of influencing world opinion in the Soviet Union's favor. And both men had agreed to continue their dialogue. Geneva was a beginning, not an end, to this new phase of Soviet-American détente. "I'm convinced that we are headed in the right direction," Reagan said.

BEGINNING OF THE END

The Americans, underestimating the Soviet Union's internal woes, viewed Gorbachev's flexibility as evidence that their high-pressure tactics were working. After the summit, the administration stepped up its covert aid to anti-Soviet fighters in Afghanistan.

When Gorbachev botched his response to the April 1986 disaster at the Chernobyl nuclear power plant, remaining silent about the crisis for nearly two weeks, then accusing the West of exploiting it for propaganda purposes, Reagan withdrew from the SALT II arms reduction pact.

Gorbachev complained that Reagan was undermining his reform efforts. He rumbled about canceling his visit to Washington. His unhappiness was in part designed to mollify hard-liners at home who thought glasnost and perestroika would cause nothing but trouble.

Then, with relations heading south, Gorbachev switched tactics. "An idea has come to my mind," he wrote to the president in mid-1986, "that, in

Both Reagan and Gorbachev were media-savvy leaders who understood the importance of performing for the press. The hordes of photographers seemed happy to get their shots.

the very near future, we have a quick one-on-one meeting, let us say in Iceland, or London, maybe just for one day, to engage in a strictly confidential, private and frank discussion." Reagan accepted, and chose Iceland.

"This is not a summit," Reagan declared before leaving for Reykjavik. He really didn't know what it was or quite what to expect. Perhaps it was an elaborate setup, a world platform from which Gorbachev could attack the United States. At the time, Reagan was also juggling other problems. A Nicaraguan soldier had just shot down a cargo plane that was ferrying supplies to the Contras. "There was no connection with the U.S. government at all," Secretary of State George Shultz assured reporters. Behind the scenes, the president's national security apparatus braced for the exposure of the Iran-Contra connection.

Reagan seemed sluggish when Gorbachev sat down across from him with a briefcase bulging with documents on October 11, 1986. He stared out the window, fiddling with his notecards, while the general secretary laid out an amazing series of proposals. "We came with nothing to offer and had offered nothing," a befuddled Reagan aide remembered. "We merely sat there while the Soviets unwrapped their gifts." Gorbachev matched the 50 percent cut in nuclear weapons that Reagan had suggested a few years earlier. Further, he was willing to remove all intermediate-range missiles from Europe so long as the Americans did the same. No Soviet leader had ever offered anything like that.

REAGAN AND GORBACHEV
1985–1988
TIMELINE

MARCH 11, 1985 Russian president Konstantin Chernenko dies and is succeeded by fifty-four-year-old Mikhail Gorbachev.

NOVEMBER 16–19, 1985 Reagan and Gorbachev meet for the Geneva summit. Reagan suggests a bilateral 50 percent reduction in nuclear arms, but the two leaders fail to reach agreement after arguing about Reagan's Strategic Defense Initiative (SDI).

OCTOBER 11, 1986 Gorbachev and Reagan meet in Reykjavik, Iceland. After a promising start, no agreement is reached and the summit is considered a failure due to a stalemate about SDI.

JUNE 12, 1987 Reagan delivers a speech at the Brandenburg Gate in West Berlin, imploring Gorbachev to "tear down this wall" and to bring liberty to the Soviet Union and Eastern Europe.

OCTOBER 30, 1987 Reagan and Gorbachev announce the upcoming U.S.-Soviet summit in Washington, D.C.

DECEMBER 8, 1987 Gorbachev visits Washington, D.C., for a summit with Reagan. The two leaders sign the INF Treaty, which eliminates 4 percent of both countries' nuclear arsenals.

APRIL 4, 1988 The Soviet Union agrees to withdraw all troops from Afghanistan by February 15, 1989.

MAY 29, 1988 President Reagan makes his first visit to Moscow. He hosts a dinner with dissidents at the U.S. Embassy and speaks to students at Moscow State University.

DECEMBER 7, 1988 Reagan, Gorbachev and President-Elect George H. W. Bush appear together at Governors Island, New York.

The non-summit flew forward at a breathtaking pace. By the end of the day, both parties had agreed to destroy all their nuclear weapons over the next ten years. "We can eliminate them," Gorbachev cheered. "Let's do it!" George Shultz interjected. Reagan had nearly realized his dream.

Then Gorbachev raised SDI. The 1972 Anti-Ballistic Missile Treaty permitted research and laboratory-based testing of space-based missile defense systems. It barred actual trial runs in space. Gorbachev wanted confirmation that the Americans would never take SDI beyond the laboratory stage. Reagan held firm. He believed that SDI would be deployed within months. In reality it was nowhere close to readiness, and probably never would be. Neither man could break through the

impasse. A single word, "laboratory," had derailed the greatest arms reduction in human history.

"There's still time, Mr. President," Gorbachev pleaded as Reagan headed for his car. "We could go back inside to the bargaining table."

"I think not," Reagan replied.

"Mr. President, you have missed the unique chance of going down in history as a great president who paved the way for nuclear disarmament," Gorbachev continued.

"That applies to both of us."

Reagan shut the door. "Goddammit, we were *that* close to an agreement," he told Shultz.

"Reagan is clinging to the SDI as a means to avoid war," Margaret Thatcher barked. "He's dreaming!" Despite such frustration, Reykjavik

Reagan arrived in Reykjavik with low expectations for the summit. Instead, he found himself within a hairbreadth of eliminating the nuclear stockpiles of both the United States and the Soviet Union.

Reagan never realized his dream of a nuclear-free world, but the boundless optimist hoped his successors might complete the work he had begun.

marked the beginning of the end of the Cold War. Reagan's famous June 1987 speech at Berlin's Brandenburg Gate, where he ordered Gorbachev to "tear down this wall," made for good television. However, it was the general secretary's domestic economic problems, along with rising dissatisfaction from rebels such as Boris Yeltsin, that forced him to set a withdrawal date from Afghanistan and to inform Soviet satellites in Eastern Europe that the Red Army would no longer intervene in their affairs.

Gorbachev, as promised, visited Washington, D.C., in 1987. After charming the American press, he and Reagan signed a treaty abolishing intermediate-range nukes. This represented only a tiny fraction of the superpowers' stockpiles, but the agreement nevertheless held tremendous symbolic value. The next year Reagan received a standing ovation from students at Moscow State University.

A reporter asked whether the Soviet Union was still an evil empire.

"No," Reagan answered. "I was talking about another time, another era."

Reagan and Gorbachev needed each other. Reagan's foreign policy victories boosted his approval ratings in the face of domestic scandals.

"Tear down this wall," Reagan demanded at Berlin's Brandenburg Gate. His 1987 speech received little attention at the time but assumed greater importance in retrospect.

Who could have imagined such a staunch anticommunist visiting Moscow on a goodwill trip?

And Gorbachev, burdened with a fading economy and attacks from his political left and right, could not liberalize the ailing Soviet system without assurances that change would improve relations with the United States.

By the time Gorbachev joined Reagan for that final photo op at the Statue of Liberty, it was clear that these two men had altered the world's direction. In part, they were prisoners of history who reacted to forces beyond their control. At the same time, they did their best to nudge those forces down peaceful paths. Ronald Reagan did not end the Cold War—no single person could make such a claim—but his determination and conviction helped pave the way toward a new era.

THERE IS ONE SIGN THE SOVIETS CAN MAKE THAT WOULD BE UNMISTAKABLE, THAT WOULD ADVANCE DRAMATICALLY THE CAUSE OF FREEDOM AND PEACE.
GENERAL SECRETARY GORBACHEV, IF YOU SEEK PEACE / IF YOU SEEK PROSPERITY FOR THE SOVIET UNION AND EASTERN EUROPE / IF YOU SEEK LIBERALIZATION! COME HERE, TO THIS GATE.
MR. GORBACHEV, OPEN THIS GATE.
MR. GORBACHEV, TEAR DOWN THIS WALL.
I UNDERSTAND THE FEAR OF WAR AND THE PAIN OF DIVISION THAT AFFLICT THIS CONTINENT / AND I PLEDGE TO YOU MY COUNTRY's EFFORTS TO HELP OVERCOME THESE BURDENS. TO BE SURE, WE IN THE WEST MUST RESIST SOVIET EXPANSION. SO WE MUST MAINTAIN DEFENSES OF UNASSAILABLE STRENGTH. YET WE SEEK PEACE. SO WE MUST STRIVE TO REDUCE ARMS ON BOTH SIDES.

Reagan's speech card from his remarks at Brandenburg Gate.

"Behind me stands a wall that encircles the free sectors of this city, part of a vast system of barriers that divides the entire continent of Europe . . . Standing before the Brandenburg Gate, every man is a German, separated from his fellow men. Every man is a Berliner, forced to look upon a scar . . . As long as this gate is closed, as long as this scar of a wall is permitted to stand, it is not the German question alone that remains open, but the question of freedom for all mankind . . . General Secretary Gorbachev, if you seek peace—if you seek prosperity for the Soviet Union and Eastern Europe—if you seek liberalization: come here to this gate. Mr. Gorbachev, open this gate. Mr. Gorbachev, tear down this wall."

—RWR, remarks on East-West relations, Brandenburg Gate, West Berlin, Germany, June 12, 1987

CHAPTER 10

THE LAST ACT

"REAGAN STOOD WITHIN REACH OF PRESIDENTIAL GREATNESS. TIME AND AGAIN . . . HE HAD STRUGGLED AGAINST CIRCUMSTANCE AND BENT IT TO HIS WILL."

—EDMUND MORRIS

"WALTER LIPPMANN ONCE SAID OF CHARLES DE GAULLE THAT HIS GREATNESS WAS NOT BECAUSE DE GAULLE WAS IN FRANCE BUT BECAUSE FRANCE WAS IN DE GAULLE. SIMILARLY, THE GREATNESS OF REAGAN WAS THAT HE CARRIED A SHINING VISION OF AMERICA INSIDE HIM."

—LOU CANNON, REAGAN BIOGRAPHER

Mr. President, the world is quiet today." Reagan's national security advisor Colin Powell spoke these words to his boss on January 20, 1989, the day George Herbert Walker Bush replaced him in the Oval Office. On that day, Reagan never expected to have to manage a crisis. Nevertheless, Powell's brief report was reassuring. Although Reagan believed in the basic goodness of individual people, he also knew that evil existed, and

On January 20, 1989, eight years after becoming president, Ronald Reagan left office, passing the reins of power to George H. W. Bush. On the steps of a waiting helicopter, Reagan saluted crisply and departed Washington, D.C., for California.

On his last morning in office, President Reagan made one final visit to the Oval Office.

left unchecked and unopposed could wreak havoc. In his eight years in office, critics had accused him of saber rattling, and supporters had lauded him for his peace proposals. He did, after all, deliver both the "Evil Empire" speech and the Pointe du Hoc address, but both expressed his deeply held views of people and governments.

Shortly after Powell departed, Reagan left the Oval Office for the last time as president of the United States. At the door, he looked back once more, back to the desk where he had signed bills into law and planned initiatives that altered the world. "Then I was gone," he later wrote.

A TRIP HOME

At eleven o'clock he departed the White House, riding to the Capitol with the president-elect for the

official transfer of power. At noon Bush was inaugurated as the forty-first president. After all the official ceremonies concluded, George and Barbara Bush walked Ronald and Nancy Reagan under the dome of the Capitol to the east side of the building, where a helicopter was waiting to take them to Andrews Field. From there, they would fly to their home in California in the plane that had been *Air Force One* during his years in office.

The pilot had a surprise for the Reagans— one last gift, really, from an appreciative nation. Without telling them, he circled the Capitol. From the sky Reagan viewed the same sight he had seen from the Capitol's inaugural stand eight years before. "Beneath us was the spectacular panorama that had been our neighborhood: The Washington Monument, the Lincoln and Jefferson Memorials, and now the bands and floats of the inaugural parade—and, everywhere on this day, huge crowds. Everything pointed to the marvel of our system of government and the ease with which it exercised the peaceful transition of power."

Dropping lower, the pilot circled the White House with its "green lawn and sparkling fountains."

"Look, honey, there's our little shack," Reagan said to his wife.

Upon his arrival at Andrews Air Force Base, he reviewed the troops, shook hands with each, listened while a military band played the national anthem, and then got into the plane with Nancy by his side. One person who had stood faithfully by

After the inauguration of President Bush, Ronald and Nancy Reagan boarded a helicopter at the Capitol for a short flight to Andrews Field, where they took a plane to California.

Before they reached Andrews Field, however, they were given a surprise in the form of a bird's-eye view of the monuments of Washington, D.C.

him for eight years was conspicuously absent. The military aide with the information the president would need in the event of a nuclear strike was gone, now attached to President Bush.

The former *Air Force One* rose into the clouds. Reagan was free from the duties of office. Free from air-to-ground telephone calls and meetings with national security advisors, free from talk of legislation with cabinet members and press conferences, free from staff briefings and the other demands of office. He was free to relax and to admire "the breathtaking beauty of our land— the emerald hills of Appalachia, the towns and small farms of the Midwest, the granite peaks of the Rockies, the rugged deserts of the Southwest, and, finally, the great metropolitan panorama of Southern California."

Reagan wrote that he looked at "the houses below and wondered about the people in those houses." But did he wonder about his own life? His own, improbable American life? Arguably no president in the twentieth century had risen from more humble circumstances. His father had a drinking problem, his parents never owned a home, and throughout Dutch's childhood and adolescence his family was the picture of downward mobility. He loved sports and played games with abandon, but was not a gifted athlete. He was an indifferent

Reagan in the cockpit on his way to California from Washington, D.C. On the trip back home, Reagan studied the beauty of the country he loved—its small towns and cities, plains and mountains, forests and deserts. He wondered about the people in the houses below.

student in high school and college, but was well liked by his classmates. He loved the world of show business, but never reached the top. But if 80 percent of success is just showing up, Dutch Reagan showed up 100 percent of the time, smiling and with his lines memorized.

THE WORK OF A LIFETIME

People often misjudged him. When he went into politics, critics wrote him off as a failed actor who, they never forgot to write, had been upstaged by a chimpanzee in *Bedtime for Bonzo*. Those barbs never seemed to faze him in the slightest. When he was elected president and went to Washington, Democratic Speaker of the House Tip O'Neill warned him that he was now playing in the "major leagues" and his "minor league" stuff might not get the job done. Reagan smiled, and before Tip knew it, his political opponent had pushed through two budget bills. What happened, one of O'Neill's Boston constituents wanted to know? "I'm getting the shit whaled out of me," the Speaker answered.

Over the years, Reagan had learned that there were worse things than being misjudged. He had a sense that the elites often misjudged the common people, and he always considered himself as one of the people. He probably thought of himself as the star in a Frank Capra movie, maybe Longfellow Deeds in *Mr. Deeds Goes to Town* or Jefferson Smith in *Mr. Smith Goes to Washington*. His strengths were those of average Americans, his voice was their voice. In his farewell address to the nation,

he denied he was "the Great Communicator." "I wasn't a great communicator, but I communicated great things, and they didn't spring full bloom from my brow, they came from the heart of a great nation—from our experience, our wisdom, and our beliefs in the principles that have guided us for two centuries. They called it the Reagan revolution. Well, I'll accept that, but for me it always seemed more like a great rediscovery, a rediscovery of our values and our common sense."

Flying over America, did he reflect upon the accomplishments of that Reagan revolution? Did he consider how history bent to his will? Beginning in his third year in office, the national economy took flight, experiencing the longest peacetime growth spurt in history. Economists and historians argue about what role his policies played in the economic boom—and indeed, exactly who participated in it—but it took place during his watch. In the last months of the Carter administration, inflation had reached 12 percent, interest rates 21 percent, and unemployment 7 percent. The "misery index"—a combination of unemployment and inflation—had climbed to a painful 20 points. As Reagan flew to California, inflation was down to 4.4 percent, the prime interest rate to 9.3 percent, and unemployment to 5.4 percent. The misery index had fallen to a more acceptable 10 points. The economic improvement had also spurred the creation of some 18.4 million jobs, and the real income of every economic class in the country improved. Yes, the wealthy became far wealthier, and the economic

In 1989, one year after Reagan departed the White House, and just two years after challenging Gorbachev to "tear down this wall," the Berlin Wall was demolished by liberated East and West Germans, ending years of division and Soviet oppression.

benefits were not shared equally or proportionately, but after a decade of decline and malaise, the "Reagan recovery" was assuredly an improvement.

Reagan's accomplishments in foreign affairs were even more remarkable and lasting. The relationship he forged with Mikhail Gorbachev changed the world. Within a year after Reagan left office, Poland, Hungary, East Germany, Czechoslovakia, Bulgaria, and Romania broke away from the Soviet orbit and held free elections. Symbolizing this seismic shift, in early November 1989, East and West Germans tore down the Berlin Wall. Reagan's 1987 challenge to Gorbachev to "tear down this wall" had been an important step in the path toward the momentous event. In

the early 1990s, the Soviet Union itself was torn down, with many of its component republics opting for independence. The Cold War, the central foreign-policy reality of Reagan's political career, was over. The Soviet Union's Marxist-Leninist dream ended, as Reagan predicted, "on the ash heap of history."

Reagan watched those events unfold as a private citizen. Occasionally he appeared in public to make a well-compensated speech, and he continued to support political causes and to endorse legislation. In 1992 he established the Ronald Reagan Freedom Award, the highest civilian honor bestowed by a private foundation. Given to "those who have made monumental and lasting contributions to the cause of freedom worldwide," the award has gone to some of the most important world leaders, including Mikhail Gorbachev, Colin Powell, Margaret Thatcher, and Lech Walesa, as well as to Bob Hope and Billy Graham.

INTO THE SUNSET

Reagan's last major public appearance occurred on April 27, 1994, when he attended the funeral of Richard Nixon. Together with President Bill Clinton and the other living former U.S. presidents—Gerald Ford, Jimmy Carter, and George H. W. Bush— he listened as the Reverend Billy Graham called Nixon "one of the most misunderstood men, and . . . one of the greatest men of the century."

At the service, however, Reagan seemed oddly distracted, as if he had turned down his hearing aid or was watching a silent movie that lacked subtitles. People who knew him speculated that something was wrong.

Even before then his health had begun to decline. His body was still hale and hardy, and he enjoyed rides at his ranch, walks on the beach, and rounds of golf, but his memory had started to slip. He forgot the names of friends he had known for decades and experienced periodic confusion. Some people close to him believed his problems resulted from a riding mishap. On July 4, 1989, while vacationing at a friend's ranch in the Mexican state of Sonora, just across the border from Arizona,

Ronald Reagan made his last major public appearance at the 1994 funeral of Richard Nixon. In Nixon's hometown of Yorba Linda, California, Reagan joined President Bill Clinton and former presidents George H. W. Bush, Jimmy Carter, and Gerald Ford.

In 1988 President Reagan and the First Lady posed for a photograph on the White House's South Lawn. Their love for each other was obvious. Ron wrote letters to Nancy almost daily.

1994 the Mayo Clinic team reexamined Reagan and confirmed their diagnosis, prompting him to take a brave, decisive step.

All his adult life, Reagan had been a letter writer. He wrote hundreds of letters and notes to Nancy. His letters to his wife were touching expressions of respect, devotion, and love, often decorated by pen or pencil drawings and doodles. One note written on White House stationery simply said:

> I love you
>
> I love you
>
> I love you
>
> I love you
>
> I love you
>
> I love you
>
> I love you
>
> I love you
>
> I love you
>
> And besides that—
>
> I love you

After his Alzheimer's diagnosis was reconfirmed, he wrote a different sort of love letter. Handwritten in his distinctive, cramped style, it was addressed to "My Fellow Americans." It began with the simple admission: "I have recently been told that I am one of the millions of Americans who will be afflicted with Alzheimer's Disease." There was no sense that he felt sorry for himself, just the hope that his announcement would raise awareness about the disease.

Edmund Morris, the historian who had been chosen to write a biography of Reagan and given

he had been thrown off a horse, suffering a brain contusion that required surgery. That fall may have contributed to his cognitive troubles. But clearly the issues were more serious.

In 1993 he underwent a series of tests at the Mayo Clinic and was diagnosed with Alzheimer's disease, the most common source of dementia. A degenerative disease, Alzheimer's usually begins by affecting the patient's short-term memory. As it progresses it may cause language problems, disorientation, mood swings, and behavioral issues. In

Nov. 5, 1994

My Fellow Americans,

I have recently been told that I am one of the millions of Americans who will be afflicted with Alzheimer's Disease.

Upon learning this news, Nancy and I had to decide whether as private citizens we would keep this a private matter or whether we would make this news known in a public way.

In the past Nancy suffered from breast cancer and I had my cancer surgeries. We found through our open disclosures we were able to raise public awareness. We were happy that as a result many more people underwent testing.

They were treated in early stages and able to return to normal, healthy lives.

So now, we feel it is important to share it with you. In opening our hearts, we hope this might promote greater awareness of this condition. Perhaps it will encourage a clearer understanding of the individuals and families who are affected by it.

At the moment I feel just fine. I intend to live the remainder of the years God gives me on this earth doing the things I have always done. I will continue to share life's journey with my beloved Nancy and my family. I plan to enjoy the great outdoors and stay in touch with my friends and supporters.

Unfortunately, as Alzheimer's Disease progresses, the family often bears a heavy burden. I only wish there was some way I could spare Nancy from this painful experience. When the time comes I am confident that with your help she will face it with faith and courage.

In closing let me thank you, the American people for giving me the great honor of allowing me to serve as your President. When the Lord calls me home, whenever that may be, I will leave with the greatest love for this country of ours and eternal optimism for its future.

I now begin the journey that will lead me into the sunset of my life. I know that for America there will always be a bright dawn ahead.

Thank you, my friends. May God always bless you.

Sincerely,
Ronald Reagan

Ronald Reagan died on June 5, 2004. Americans said their official good-bye to him a few days later.

singular access to him, saw a facsimile of the letter in the newspaper. "For the first time in my life I felt love for Ronald Reagan, and overpowering sadness," he wrote.

A month later, Morris visited Reagan in the former president's skyscraper suite in Los Angeles. He immediately sensed the change in Dutch—the way he smiled without remembering, the "patch of silvery stubble" on the chin of the man who was always so perfectly groomed, and the hesitant, distracted manner in which he spoke. The conversation was awkward, meandering toward no real end.

Finally Reagan led Morris over to a framed picture on the wall. The writer thought it might be the so-called Five Presidents photograph, taken at Richard Nixon's funeral, but it wasn't. It was a watercolor of a river scene, a place that Morris knew well, and Reagan knew even better.

"This is where I was a lifeguard for seven summers," Reagan said. "I saved seventy-seven lives.

And you know, none of 'em ever thanked me!"

Morris wrote that at that moment, he did not feel the true presence of Reagan beside him, but wondered if perhaps Reagan did feel the presence of the Rock River—the cold of the water and the swirl of the eddies—as he took in the painting.

By the beginning of 1995 Reagan had left the public gaze, his privacy scrupulously protected by Nancy. Newspapers reported certain milestones, such as when he became only the third former president to reach the age of ninety, and noted signs of his failing health, such as the time he fell and broke his hip. But as a vital force with a healthy public presence, he had disappeared.

On June 5, 2004, Ronald Reagan died of pneumonia at the age of ninety-three. He had lived longer than any other previous president, and he had lived fully. From Tampico and Dixon to Hollywood and Washington, D.C., his had been a uniquely American life.

Ronald Reagan's last years were clouded by Alzheimer's disease. But his image in the minds of millions of Americans is clear and strong, and his optimism and faith in his country changed the world.

IMAGE CREDITS

ABOUT THE AUTHORS

Randy Roberts is Distinguished Professor of History at Purdue University. His primary research area is American history and culture. He is the author of *Jack Dempsey: The Manassa Mauler*; *Papa Jack: Jack Johnson and the Era of White Hopes*; and *Joe Louis: Hard Times Man*. His most recent books are *A Team for America: The Army-Navy Game That Rallied a Nation* and *Rising Tide: Bear Bryant, Joe Namath, and Dixie's Last Quarter*. Roberts has served frequently as a consultant and on-camera commentator for PBS, HBO, and the History Channel. He lives in Lafayette, Indiana, with his wife Marjie.

David Welky is a Professor of History at the University of Central Arkansas who grew up during the Reagan era. A specialist in twentieth-century American history, he is the author of *Marching Across the Color Line: A. Philip Randolph and Civil Rights in the World War II Era*, *The Thousand-Year Flood: The Ohio-Mississippi Disaster of 1937*, and *The Moguls and the Dictators: Hollywood and the Coming of World War II*, among other books.